THE JOYS OF COUNTRY STRIFE

THE JOYS OF COUNTRY STRIFE

June Baker

ATHENA PRESS
LONDON

ISBN 1 84401 613 7

First Published 2006 by
ATHENA PRESS
Queen's House, 2 Holly Road
Twickenham TW1 4EG
United Kingdom

Printed for Athena Press

Foreword

I used to work primarily as a secretary in one of the big five banks, filling in any spare time from dictation, typing and filing with ledger work, hand-written statements and adding up columns of figures in my head and fingers; no adding machines around in those days. It was the 30th of June and the half-yearly balance was to be completed by midnight. We met the deadline at eight o'clock.

To celebrate, Teresa the junior and I decided that we would like to go dancing at the Old Mill just outside Bath, which was a very popular rendezvous with all our friends. So, we arranged for a taxi to pick us up from the bank, wait outside our homes whilst we changed into clothes more attractive than 'bank working garb', then to take us to the station to catch a train to Bath, then another taxi to the Old Mill. Little did I know this was where my future was destined to take a complete change of direction.

Many of our friends were there and of course a number of unknowns one of whom was talking to a very good friend whom I often danced with at our local community centre.

'Hello,' I said to my friend.

'Good to see you,' he replies. 'Let me introduce you to my cousin.' We shook hands.

'Would you like to dance?' said the cousin, whose name was Malcolm.

'I'd love to,' I smiled. He was an excellent dancer –

quickstep and foxtrot no problem, even rock and roll (a new dance craze). We seemed to be talking quite a lot as well on so many different subjects.

Then he said, 'Would you like to see my otter skin?' This was certainly a bit different to 'would you like to see my etchings?' I hesitated.

'Where is it?'

'In the back of my Bradford van in the car park.' Again I hesitated. This approach was a bit advanced for me but… I was very curious. He seemed to be a very nice sort of person and I knew his cousin very well.

'All right,' I said, 'I'd love to.' After all, I was not far from the main group; but I did say to Teresa very discreetly, 'I'm going out to the car park to see an otter skin.'

'A what?' she exclaimed.

'An otter skin, and if I'm not back in ten minutes come and fetch me or send out a search party,' I laughed. It was a lovely June evening, not far off midnight; a full moon shone in all its glory amongst the stars. We walked across the car park towards a Bradford van. Malcolm unlocked the back doors, reached inside and pulled out what looked like a roll of hair and leather. He gave it a shake and the bundle unravelled into a long-tailed, beautiful, soft, furry animal skin. It was, or had been a full-grown otter. Malcolm explained how he had been driving home one night when this otter had run across the road right in front of him; he felt a very soft bump, bump. He stopped immediately and ran round to see how badly hurt the otter was – fortunately, in a way, the animal was stone dead.

Not a spot of blood anywhere. So Malcolm put the creature in the back of the Bradford and drove back to his digs. The following day he skinned the animal and pegged the skin on to an old door and treated it with several applications of saltpetre and alum; the skin when cured was beautifully soft and supple.

We drifted back into the Old Mill just as the leader of the small band said 'Take your partners for the last waltz'… The evening was over… but it was the start to a very happy, forever-interesting life together. We were married within a year. Now, many, many years later, we are still doing great and interesting things together, sharing our achievement with our three children, now grown up with children of their own. Who would have thought an otter skin would have been the catalyst for so many years of happiness? And so to The Joys of Country Strife…

Chapter One

You've never seen a house like it – the little cottage must have clung to the side of that wet Welsh hill for well over two centuries, with almost as many coats of whitewash peeling from its lumpy walls. It was certainly no fairy castle. There were traces of brown and green paint to be seen hanging on to the window frames and door; a rusty iron and brass bed-head gate spanned the gap between the cottage and the crumbling wall which surrounded the tiny front garden. I think the wall had been built to keep the sun from the windows when it dared to shine into that green, misty valley.

Malcolm and I had looked at many houses and cottages and studied reams of estate agents' literature. Consequently, we were becoming quite adept at translating fiction into fact. 'Peaceful and secluded' meant two miles down a mud track, in the middle of a wood, and the nearest shop five miles away.

'Enchanting olde world cottage' – a two up and two down, no electricity or piped water. 'Easily maintained house and garden' – all rooms eight by ten with parking space in the garden for a pram or dog kennel.

This property had eluded the estate agent's pen, or perhaps even they had been reluctant to put it in writing. Malcolm had been told about the cottage by a friend (some friend) who had obviously whiled away some time in an estate agent's office. I distinctly remember him saying 'a dear little cottage' – he was right there; it would cost a small fortune to make it resemble anything like 'a dear little cottage' – 'by the side of a road (even if there were weeds growing in the middle of it) and some land'; two fields behind the house on a one in three incline. Four fields in front of the house, covered in rushes. Every landowner's dream.

'Let's go and have a look inside,' said Malcolm.

'What about all those bulls?' I wailed, as I eyed what I thought to be about twenty very lively bulls cavorting around the field and yard in front of the house.

'Those aren't bulls,' Malcolm laughed, 'they've been castrated. Castration makes them grow big and fat and have lovely docile natures.'

'Well, that one over there doesn't look very docile to me. Look at his ears all sticking up in the air and he's got big, bulgy eyes, and why isn't he eating grass or fooling around like the others? I bet they missed that one,' I moaned.

I had been brought up in a town and I do not like cows. Any cow that hasn't an undercarriage that looks like an upturned kitchen stool must be a bull, as far as I'm concerned.

'It's probably the only steer that has noticed us and, as they're very curious animals, he wants to have a good look at anything new on the scene,' explained my dear husband.

With that he was over the gate and making for the 'dear little cottage'. Not wanting to be left behind, I heaved my six-months-pregnant hulk over the gate at the hinge end (I wasn't completely ignorant of country ways) and walked warily across the yard, eyeing the 'bulls' with great respect, wondering to myself if they did charge, whether I should race back to the gate or make for the iron and brass bed-head.

The house had been empty for two years, and leaves

from two autumns had blown under the front door and carpeted the tiny quarry-tiled hall. There was a room on the left of the hall – paper hung from the walls, the skirting boards had been painted at some time in the long distant past in a delicate shade of ginger-brown, the door a murky bottle green. The tiny fireplace, which crouched halfway along one wall, was hardly big enough to hold three small pieces of coal. The room on the right of the hall, though with the same decor (ginger and bottle green), was considerably larger. This room however was dominated by a huge black range, complete with bread oven, which spanned three quarters the length of one wall. The ceiling made of six-inch planks of dark stained oak did not make things any brighter.

I walked down the little passage which led from the hall to the two rooms at the back of the house, both only six feet wide and twelve feet long. The room on the left had obviously been the scullery and still had big stone slabs the full length of one wall, which hardly left any space to squeeze past. The other narrow room (judging by the wallpaper) had been used for sleeping accommodation – you could hardly call it a bedroom.

Upstairs next. I mounted the narrow staircase which opened straight into one large bedroom; there was a brown door which led into a smaller bedroom. And that was it. Obviously, this was the 'enchanting, olde worlde cottage' type property – two up, two down, no water or electricity.

Malcolm was nowhere to be seen. After gingerly crossing the yard, I found him in the pigsties adjoining the cottage, grunting happily to himself. He was apparently quite at home.

'This is just what we want,' he enthused. Did we? I

was sure in my mind that we had wanted just a simple modern three-bedroomed house, with flower borders, a vegetable patch and nice neighbours. It just shows how wrong one can be.

Malcolm broke in on my thoughts. 'We could pump water from the spring or dig a well. Electricity has been brought as far as the gate – it wouldn't take much to have the power brought into the house; easy enough to put in some power plugs and lighting. A spot of paint around the place and it could really look quite nice. The out-buildings are good; we could keep a few pigs and I reckon that we could feed a few steers on those fields.' He wasn't even out of breath.

I took a long look at my husband. We had been mar-ried just a year and had spent it very happily living in a fairly comfortable flat in the market town of Carmarthen. We had sailed, played tennis and been able to swim in the lovely unspoilt bays of West Wales. Now I was pregnant and we were looking for a larger, more permanent home. Changes I knew were sure to come, but the idea of living right in the heart of the country was a change for which I had not bargained. To Malcolm, a farmer's son, it was the ideal.

'Well, what do you think?' Malcolm was waiting for my answer. I hesitated.

'Well, it isn't quite the place I imagined that we'd move into...'

'But you don't mind giving it a try. Do you?' he asked. I just could not let the light of my life see that my pioneering spirit was at a very low ebb. So I slowly nodded my agreement. Decision made. That was it. Within twenty-four hours we had paid six months' rent in advance, invaded the local shops for paint, turps, scrapers, brushes, sandpaper, a wheelbarrow, a shovel and a hurricane lamp, and were back at the cottage with our old Bradford van practically bursting at the seams.

The solicitor who was involved with the letting of the cottage told us that we could make any changes to the property that we thought were necessary to improve it, but at our expense. Apparently the property was in a trust to four members of a family who could not agree on the fate of the cottage. So it was agreed that they would take rent from us until such time as they could come to some arrangement between themselves, but they were prepared to let us have the cottage for a minimum of three years.

So we were ready for action. We decided that we would spend the next three months putting the little house in some sort of order and actually move into Fronlas (the name of our newly-acquired property) in April, after the baby was born. It was now January. Our first job was to contact the local electricity board and ask them to bring a power cable into the house from their transformer, which in due course they did. Meanwhile, that first week after we had finished our day's work, Malcolm, assistant manager in a large dairy producing many different types of cheese, and me, a secretary in an auctioneer's office – we would bump our way along the twisty lanes to make our olde worlde cottage enchanting. By the light of the hurricane lamp, Malcolm fitted light switches, power plugs and junction boxes. By candlelight I shovelled umpteen barrow loads of stone and slate from the old scullery. I was to learn very early in my married life that work was good for me, pregnant or otherwise.

Clearly, our biggest problem was going to be the water supply. It would appear that all previous residents had hauled water from a spring some fifty metres from the cottage. So, either we could install a pump or, if we could strike water behind and above the house, we could gravity feed it into a tank in the roof. We had the luck, or so we thought, of being told about a local carpenter who could divine water with a hazel twig. We asked him if he would walk the field on the bank behind the house to see what the chances were. He arrived one Saturday afternoon – he looked just like the toymaker in *Pinocchio* – white hair, blue eyes, rosy cheeks and a pair of spectacles which just balanced on the end of his nose.

With a hazel twig held firmly in his gnarled hands, he walked the field for about two hours. Every now and then the stick would twist and dive to the ground. If there really was water under every spot the stick touched, we must be right over a large subterranean lake with enough water to supply the whole of Wales. Unfortunately, the stick never came down on the same spot twice. Nevertheless, we marked a place where Dick the carpenter-cum-water-diviner assured us that we would find a good flow of water probably just five feet from the surface.

We were very excited about starting our well – anyone would think that we were digging for oil, not water. It was a bit late to start digging that afternoon, so we decided that we would start first thing in the morning, particularly as we were going out with some friends that evening. They seemed to think that we were quite mad wanting to live in the country, let alone digging a well for water. Perhaps we were mad, but it certainly made life more interesting.

The next morning we arrived at Fronlas just after nine o'clock armed with a strong spade and a camera. I wanted a photograph of Malcolm digging out the first spadeful of earth, which hopefully would eventually lead to a good supply of water. After taking a couple of shots of Malcolm attacking that Welsh hillside and watching the first few turfs being tossed aside, I went down to the house to get on with the painting.

About an hour later Malcolm was at the door saying that he would have to go into town to borrow a drill. Apparently after digging out two feet of earth he had struck slate and, obviously, he would need something more powerful than a spade. Luckily, we had a builder friend who could let us borrow a small electric drill. Within an hour and a half, Malcolm was back with a drill, a transformer and about one hundred yards of cable and had plugged in and started frilling out the slate, which appeared to be stacked end on, like the burnt pages of a telephone directory. Unfortunately, the bit head would only dig in about an inch at a time. It took ages to work across the whole area; I suppose the hole was about two feet by three feet.

We were lucky that the electricity board had connected us to the power supply two days earlier. That first day Malcolm inched his way down about a foot below ground level. Obviously, this was going to be a long, slow job. Painting, by contrast, was quite quick and it was rewarding to see that awful ginger paint being submerged with fresh, white undercoat and finished with a brilliant, shiny gloss.

During the next two months, having finished work at the estate agents' office, I completed the painting of the cottage and Malcolm put the finishing touches to the kitchen and bathroom. Our nest was complete except for water. We were down to fifteen feet and still the water only dripped off the sides of the well. Where was that vast water supply that we were led to believe lay just five feet below the surface? I hated to see Malcolm disappear down that tiny hole and not be able to help him at all.

I could not even haul up the buckets that Malcolm filled with shale as he worked across the base of the well because as the bucket banged against the sides, small pieces of slate were dislodged. These could gather quite a speed by the time they reached Malcolm's head, which could have given him a headache that he could do well without. So, he was forced to carry up the ladder each bucket that we had dropped into the well, up to the surface.

I hoped that it would not be too long before we found a decent water supply, as it was now the beginning of April and soon we would be wanting to move into our little house.

Meanwhile, I had decided that I wanted a clothes horse and Malcolm had convinced me that I would enjoy making my own, even though I did not know one end of a wood chisel from the other. Nevertheless, I sawed up the wood into the right lengths, gouged out joints, wrapped the appropriate pieces with webbing and was happily engaged in smoothing down my handiwork with sandpaper when I had a peculiar sensation in my back. The baby was not due for another two days, so I did not think that it could be anything to do with McNabs, as we had christened the bump. However, twenty minutes later I again felt the same sensation. Malcolm came in just after it happened a third time, so I told him about it and asked him if he thought by any chance it might be the baby that was causing the odd twinge. That was obviously the joke of the week.

'You don't have pains in your back when you're having a baby. Not unless you are deformed,' he laughed. That was not so difficult to believe either, I thought, looking at the great bulge that hid McNabs.

'No,' Malcolm continued, 'I expect you've been bending over that clothes horse too long. Anyway, we had better get cleaned up; we're due at Fred and Nina's for supper in just under an hour.'

So we went back to the flat, made ourselves a little more respectable and presented ourselves on our friends' doorstep. We had a lovely meal then decided to play cards. Just like an alarm clock, the tickle continued every twenty minutes throughout the evening. Fred and Nina also thought it was quite a joke to have pains in one's back and not one's tum, so who was I to worry? By midnight, having won the princely sum of two shillings and sixpence, we decided that it was time to go home.

I woke up at three o'clock; my tickle had now moved round to my right side, every seven minutes. I woke up my beloved and suggested he telephoned the hospital to see what they advised. He came racing up the stairs about three minutes later, all excited.

'Yes, quick hurry up and get dressed; you've got to go in straight away.' I dressed as quickly as possible and started putting on eye shadow and mascara; cosmetics I only used when going to a dance.

'Come on,' my husband chided, 'you're going to the Miles Thomas maternity ward, not the Arts Ball.'

'Yes, but it's really happening at last – we're going to have a baby.' There could not have been more excitement in the air when Adam and Eve produced their firstborn. Within fifteen minutes I was ready, sitting in the car with the inevitable suitcase that accompanies all mothers to be to the maternity ward – ready to get on with the job in hand. Tucked into my washbag was a piece of tape that I had embroidered with the name 'Baker' in blue, ready for the baby due to be born. In those days this was the way that newly-born babies were identified at birth.

The old Bradford rattled to life and off we went. A full-grown hare, the colour of ripe, wet corn, stood momentarily transfixed in the beam of the headlights before tearing up the road in front of us, and just before I was sure we would draw level, it leapt into the hedge and disappeared into the safe darkness of a field.

We arrived at the hospital without further incident. A night nurse showed us into a single room and told Malcolm that he could stay for five minutes and that I must get undressed and into bed as soon as he left. The five minutes slipped by; it seemed five seconds. A quick hug and a kiss and the thought that by tomorrow night he would have a son or daughter to care for as well as a wife.

As soon as Malcolm left, I can't say I 'hopped' into bed, but I did get into it as quickly as I could. I just couldn't wait to get on with the job in hand – or should I say 'tummy'?

'How long will it be before the baby arrives?' I asked the nurse. Anyone would think it was due in on the six o'clock train.

'My, you are impatient,' she said, prodding my bump. Then, after a pause, 'A couple of hours I should think.'

Actually, it was seven o'clock the next morning before the Baker heir put in an appearance, but he was well worth waiting for, all seven and a half pounds of him. I examined him from head to toe to make sure he was all there and looked at the little face of the most important baby I had ever seen.

I watched him with an eagle eye while his blue, chain-stitched nametape was fixed around his tiny wrist. He was then taken away to be washed and tucked snugly in a warm cot.

The nurse then turned to me. 'I expect you'd like to have a sleep now?'

'I'd rather have something to eat – I'm starving.' Sleep was the last thing I wanted; I was far too excited. They seemed a little surprised but eventually produced a lunch of sausages and mash, the best I had ever tasted.

I could hardly wait for visiting time that evening to show Malcolm our newborn son. In those days no matter what time of the day or night a baby was born, the father was not allowed into the ward at any time other than the official hour. Which was very frustrating, to say the least. Needless to say, Malcolm was absolutely delighted.

I stayed in hospital for a week before returning to the flat for ten days prior to our move to Fronlas. The time passed very quickly – what with coping with Leigh, the first edition to our family, trying to pack everything into an assortment of boxes and suitcases and the endless journeys to the cottage in the old Bedford van loaded to capacity. But at last everything had been transported from the flat, including ourselves, and we were in our 'dear little cottage'.

Chapter Two

We woke the next morning to the sound of the curlew, blue skies and sunshine. What better welcome could one have to the country? It was only six o'clock but Malcolm was full of bright ideas.

'Let's go for a walk and survey our estate,' he suggested. I must say it certainly sounded very appealing. Leigh had been fed and was now sleeping peacefully and with luck would not need any attention for a couple of hours, when it would be bath time. How adaptable babies are; as long as they are fed, changed and watered at regular intervals they don't seem to notice any upheavals that affect the rest of the family – at least ours didn't at this stage.

We had a quick cup of tea and stepped out into the clearest sky and warm morning sun. First we walked to the top of the field on the bank behind the house, inspecting the well as we passed. Surface water had drained into the hole over the weekend, plus we hoped water from the spring, wherever it lay hidden; it still wasn't quite enough for a constant supply.

'I'll pump the well dry after breakfast and then carry on drilling,' said Malcolm. 'I should think if I dig out another five feet we should have enough to keep us going. Then I'll take a sample into town to be analysed, just to make sure that the water really is safe enough for us to use. It should be all right, we're high enough here so it shouldn't be contaminated in any way.'

At the moment we were hauling water in milk churns, so the sooner we had our own water supply, the better. I had soon learnt that you can use water more than once. That first week I had a graded system operating.

Soapy water first washed clothes, then the kitchen floor; it was then thrown onto the pigsty floor in an effort to make it a little cleaner, in readiness for the day that it became inhabited by the family of pigs that we were going to buy.

We walked back down the field, our boots black and shiny with the heavy dew, and into the field in front of the house. A curlew half rose right from under our feet, fluttered along the ground then dropped into the grass. Thinking that the poor creature had damaged its wing, I walked slowly towards it, whereupon it ran off in a different direction. Again I quietly followed, when suddenly it rose without effort into the morning sun shouting its beautiful ascending warning cry for all to hear.

'It must have been sitting on some eggs when we disturbed it – let's see if we can find them,' said Malcolm. Sure enough, after a five minute search we found two large eggs, just lying on the ground, not a vestige of a nest to be seen anywhere.

'They just lay them in the open and trust the colour of the eggs will be sufficient camouflage,' Malcolm explained. I must admit the off-white background and the irregular brown spots on the eggs certainly blended well with the tufty green-brown grass and the bare patches of earth.

We left the eggs and walked on down the field to the stream, which was our boundary. Carefully peering through the branches of the bushy hazels which straddled the banks, we were able to see a beautiful brown trout treading water in the safe overhang of the bank, the red spots on its side shining through the clear water like fairy lights along the bow of a ship. Daffodils nestled along the side of the stream, nodding their yellow trumpets in the early morning breeze. We meandered with the brook across two fields and then turned back to the house. We had plenty of work waiting for us – the well being top of the list. Malcolm had decided to take a week of his annual holiday so that he could finish the well and generally sort out all the odd jobs that seem to appear when moving from our flat to our Enchanting Olde Worlde Cottage.

I spent the next two days putting the house straight, even finding the right place for the cornflakes – having tried three cupboards before the final resting place was found. It was on Wednesday morning over breakfast that Malcolm nearly made me choke on the cornflakes.

'How about going into market today to see if we can buy a few steers? There's plenty of grass about; we could easily run four and still be able to make enough hay to keep them through the winter and (a slight pause) now is the best time to buy them. We might even be able to buy a sow and litter as well.'

Pigs and cows. It was beginning to sound more as if we had a ranch than a very, very small patch of seven acres of hill and marsh. Malcolm just could not wait to have some animals around the place. 'I suppose you know the type of animals to buy,' I ventured. Having only recently discovered the difference between a bull and a steer, I was in no position to offer any advice.

Apparently Herefords or Hereford-cross-Friesian would fill the bill admirably, according to my spouse.

'Anyway, it'll be a good exercise just to go into the market to get the lie of the land and if something good crops up, we'll buy it.' Despite my healthy respect for those horned, four-legged creatures, I could not help feeling excited at the prospect of buying some bullocks. The pram was slotted into the back of the Bradford and with Leigh in my arms we set off for Carmarthen.

We arrived at the market at ten o'clock; as selling did not start until half past eleven, we had plenty of time to look at the animals as they were ushered into the various pens. Arriving in huge lorries, the cows would stand at the top of the tailboard ramp, startled and surprised and no doubt relieved that their bumpy journey had at last ended. But, theirs was not to stand and stare; a sharp poke in the ribs from one of the many drovers soon had them slithering and sliding down the wooden slope, jostling each other to get into the comparative quiet of an open, iron cell for an hour or two until they were hustled into the selling ring before yet another lorry ride. For the lucky ones, a new home; for the not so lucky, the local abattoir.

We wandered from pen to pen, Malcolm taking the numbers of any steers that he particularly fancied. Suddenly, above the noise of bellowing cattle and men alike, the dull clang of a bell could be heard. 'That's the signal to let people know that selling is about to start,' said Malcolm.

'It sounds more as if the muffin man has come to town.' Ignoring my remark, Malcolm grabbed my arm and steered me towards the selling ring. Everyone in the market, it seemed, was making for the same place. We were pushed and jostled along the gangways just like the cattle a short time earlier. I wonder what they thought as they peered at us through the bars, pushing and elbowing our way to the ring.

The first two steers stumbled into the arena, their heads low, looking for an escape away from the jabbing stick of the drover.

'A couple of nice three-year-olds,' mused my husband, 'ready for slaughter though; we need something a little younger than that.'

'Well, what have we here?' shouted the auctioneer. 'A fine pair of beasts. Now, where will you start me?' That was all I understood. The words that followed seemed absolute gibberish until the hammer was brought down on the table with a triumphant thump, with the single word, 'sold'. So it continued for the next hour and a half, during which time Malcolm joined in the gibberish and bought five steers three Herefords, one Hereford-cross-Friesian and a gentle, timid, jet black Aberdeen Angus. We managed to get them all in one pen and made arrangements with the owner of a cattle lorry to take the animals to their new home. Ours.

'Well,' declared Malcolm – now the great rancher – 'we may as well look at the pigs now we're here.'

Pigs – I'd heard terrible stories about pigs, and weren't they dirty, smelly things? Upon voicing these thoughts, Malcolm said that occasionally you did get a nasty sow, but not very often; they were not dirty animals as they never fouled their beds like cows and horses; and, if they did become stinky, it was the owner's fault for not cleaning out the sties. So, when I was confronted by a pen filled with clean straw and eight pink, plump piglets, snuggled up to an equally clean mum, I thought perhaps it might not be such a bad idea after all to keep a few pigs.

In ten very quick minutes we had bought two sows

and their litters, amounting to nineteen pigs. One sow
was a pure Large White – what I would call 'the traditional pig' – with large upright ears, short, fat snout and a
big, strong, rounded body. In complete contrast was the
other sow, a Welsh cross – long droopy ears, which
covered its eyes, an equally long nose and a long narrow
back. Had they been male we would have undoubtedly
have called them Laurel and Hardy; as it was they were
'christened' Lantern Jaw and Loppy Lugs, which was not
very feminine either. But, there was nothing dainty or
refined about our two mums.

We arranged transport for our latest purchase and
decided that we had better go home and prepare things
for our new residents. During all this time, Leigh had
slept soundly in his pram as he was pushed around the
market from cow pen to pig pen, but now he was awake
and wanting his lunch.

On the way home we called at the miller's and
collected bran and some special pellets for the piglets and
their mums.

'Well, at least we don't have to buy special food for the
cattle, there is plenty of good grass available, thank
goodness,' said Malcolm. Thank goodness we had
everything practically ready for the pigs.

The sties were as clean as we could make them; we
filled two bowls with water and two with bran for each of
the two sows. In the creep feed – an area that the piglets
could walk into but the mother could not – we scattered
pellets in a small trough. Just as we were finishing a late
and hasty lunch and bedding Leigh down for his afternoon sleep, the pick-up vehicle arrived containing our
mini herd of swine. The vehicle was backed as close as
possible to the pigsty door, the remaining gap bridged by

Malcolm and myself holding pieces of corrugated zinc (I very soon learnt that this was a most essential piece of 'pig control' equipment). The tailboard of the pick-up was dropped and an old door placed against the edge of the van. The other end of the door rested on the ground; the door was then covered with straw so that the animals would not slip as they made their way to ground level. We hoped that our roofless 'tin tunnel' would lead the sows and piglets into the sties without mishap.

The two litters had been separated in the van with a large piece of chipboard – we did not want any fights on our hands. The first sow to attempt the descent was the Welsh cross; she stood at the top of the ramp, her nose in the air, ears parting sufficiently for her eyes to make a brief appearance. She looked as if she was adjusting her sight through a badly fitting pair of bifocals. She obviously was not impressed with what met her watery eyes for she made no effort to go down the ramp.

'I think she'll need a little persuasion,' said Malcolm. 'I'll take a couple of the little ones and put them in the sty. Perhaps that'll get them moving.' He deftly plucked two piglets from the pick-up; they immediately started squealing – the response from the sow was very effective and started a chain reaction which took some stopping.

She started grunting very loudly, which made the remaining piglets squeak and scurry in all directions, then started to make her way gingerly down the ramp. The activity and noise was obviously just too much for the sow on the other side of the partition, for she wriggled her large powerful nose under the loosely placed section of chipboard and tossed it over her shoulder and practically charged down the ramp, arriving at the pigsty entrance at exactly the same time as the Welsh cross sow, so that we ended up with two sows and seventeen piglets all in the same sty. Not exactly what we had in mind. However, we quickly put a piece of corrugated zinc between the two sows then gently eased the Welsh cross (Loppy Lugs) into the next pen. We found that she was much easier to manoeuvre than the Large White due to the fact that her ears covered her eyes most of the time.

Once the sows were in their separate pens, the job of sorting out the piglets was easier than I had dared hope.

Each sow inspected their new home, drank very noisily from their water bowls, waffled and blew through the barley meal in their troughs, then started to push the straw about with their noses and feet. Eventually, apparently satisfied with the result, they both flopped onto their sides and started a happy, contented rhythmic grunting. The seventeen piglets obviously recognised their respective mum's grunt, and split into two groups, each party making for their own mother through the low rail of the dividing section. Peace and order at last reigned.

Malcolm paid the van driver and we had a ten minute breather before the cattle lorry rattled to a halt on the roadside outside the cottage. I couldn't help thinking that perhaps we'd need something more than a piece of zinc corrugated or otherwise to stop six hundredweight of beef and in fact I said so. 'You'll see,' said my dear husband. 'You can normally stop a cow by standing in front of it and waving your arms, but a pig takes not a blind bit of notice. The only thing that'll stop a pig is something solid; not necessarily strong, just as long as it can't see through, round, over or under, the pig can normally be controlled.'

At that moment I was no longer concerned with how

you could funnel pigs into sties, only how I would be able to avoid being trampled by approximately two hundred mobile beef dinners. The driver reversed the lorry into the yard and then backed it into the field entrance; even when the tail board was down there was still quite a gap either side of the ramp.

'You stand that side and I'll stand on the other,' commanded my leader. Little did my leader know that I intended moving off quite smartly should any steer disobey the rules by not going where it was intended to go. I needn't have worried – once the back of the lorry had been let down and the gentle slope covered yet again with straw, the cattle needed little persuasion to come down the ramp. They slithered over the wooden struts and made straight for the open field and the lush grass that waited for them, tearing at the heavy crop as if they had not eaten for a week.

We closed the gate behind them, paid off yet another driver and decided it was time for a large cup of tea.

'Let's go and see how much water there is in the well,' Malcolm suggested as we sipped the ever-welcome cuppa. 'With a bit of luck it should be somewhere near full; we'll take a bottle and string so that we can take a sample.'

I always found it exciting going up to the well – how deep would it be, how full, how soon before we would be able to actually use its contents?

We wandered up the hill, pushed the slab of stone that covered the hole to one side and peered down. About another three feet to go, and it certainly looked nice and clear. 'Pass me the bottle and string,' said Malcolm. You can guess who had had the honour of carrying the sample bottle. He slipped the string around the neck of the bottle, pulled the knot tight and dropped the bottle into the dark chasm. A loud plop echoed up the walls as the bottle hit the water, this was followed by a series of mini explosions as the air bubbled out of the bottle to be replaced with water. I waited eagerly for the bottle to appear. Malcolm at last lifted the bottle up to the surface, the water was as clear as a million dewdrops and so cold.

'Can we taste it?' I asked. Being a real townie, I had not tasted fresh spring water before.

'It should be all right,' said Malcolm. 'The worst thing you could get would only be typhoid.' This remark was accompanied by a large grin, which quickly disappeared when I kicked him on the shin.

Anyone watching would have thought that we were about to indulge in sampling a bottle of 1927 vintage port. For the number of man hours that had gone into the digging of the well, the price would not have been far off either.

The water really was quite different from treated tap water – no doubt the low temperature helped, plus the fact that we had just puffed up the steep, sloping field to reach the well. Nevertheless, it was quite delicious.

'Why not take the sample in this afternoon? It would be great to know that everything was all right, and just think, no more water hauling.' Malcolm did not need much persuasion – water hauling was not much fun and I think he had reached the stage that twenty feet through slate was enough for anyone.

'Right. I must admit it would be marvellous to have no more digging to do.'

It was teatime by the time Malcolm returned from Carmarthen, having waited for the analyst's report. I heard the old Bradford van bubble into the yard – a very distinct sound, apparently due to it having a two stroke engine. I raced outside to find out the result of the well water. Malcolm's face was the answer – a huge grin from ear to ear. I had a great feeling of relief. I had not realised how keyed up I had been about the whole water question. The weeks of digging and hauling water had been quite a trial and in the back of our minds wondering all the time if we would have to boil the water or treat it, even if we did have a good enough supply.

A problem solved and behind us, it was time for bed. What a long day. I was beginning to feel that this farming lark could be quite hectic and we'd only just started. Thank goodness we only had seven acres. It was certainly different from the banking routine that I had followed for the three years before we were married.

Chapter Three

Time sped by and all our livestock was growing well. Leigh could now focus his eyes properly and sleep all night (a great achievement as far as I was concerned). The steers munched happily in the fields and the piglets, now eight weeks old, were getting so fat that they looked like mobile piggy banks, especially those from the Large White sow.

'It's time they were weaned and the sow taken to the boar,' said Malcolm as we watched them snoring in a neat line under the sow's udder. They certainly did not have to move far for a meal. I could cope with the weaning, but the thought of taking that huge sow anywhere did not exactly make me jump for joy.

'We'll rest the old pigsty door on the base of the Bradford, to form a ramp with corrugated zinc either side, and if the van is backed right up to the pigsty door, we should have no trouble at all.' And strangely enough, we didn't.

I climbed in beside Malcolm and held Leigh in my arms, who soon went to sleep with the gentle bumping motion of the van. We had to sit bolt upright, with little leg space, because Malcolm had put the wooden division between the sow and us as far forward as possible. We couldn't see the sow behind us as the planks of wood were nailed very close together, but we could hear her snuffling. We had driven the six miles into Carmarthen and were just passing St Peter's Church when the sow started to wriggle her long snout under the partition. Malcolm quickly put his thumb firmly on her nose and she promptly pulled her head back but, seconds later, decided to have another go. This time she pushed her whole nose under the partition and lifted it smartly onto her shoulders. I yelled at Malcolm to do something quickly; Leigh woke up and started screaming; Malcolm started to hit the sow on the nose with the Bradford's starting handle (the only 'weapon' that was available) which immediately started the sow squealing. The noise was deafening. I could almost see the squeals rising from the pink throat and bouncing off the pink, pointed tongue – my head being only five inches from the sow's. If there were people watching, I would have loved to have seen their faces, but we were too occupied to look anywhere other than at the sow.

After three sharp thumps on her supposedly sensitive nose, she eventually withdrew into the back of the van. Fortunately the partition slipped back into place. 'It's only half a mile to Pibwrlloyd, with a bit of luck we'll get there before she thinks of having another go. Anyway, if she does, hit her with this,' said Malcolm, handing me the starting handle.

The noise and tension had left me a trembling jelly; I just hoped that the sow would stay quietly in the back of the van and spend the time concentrating on how to remain standing on all fours as we drove along the last mile of twisting lanes.

At long last we drove into the yard of Pibwrlloyd, where a number of boars of various breeds were kept. Luckily, a workman was in the yard and was able to tell us into which pen the sow should go. The sow backed very slowly and sedately down the ramp as if she'd spent her life trundling up and down ramps, in and out of Bradford vans.

'There's quiet she is,' remarked the farmhand. I looked at the twenty score of docile sow that stood blinking benignly in the morning sun. I could have quite cheerfully kicked her in the rump for looking so smug. Obviously she was a classic schizophrenic – a definite Jekyll and Hyde.

'Come back in a couple of days, the boar should have wooed her successfully by then,' said the farmhand.

'Don't you want us to help you to put her into a pen?' I ventured.

'Oh no *bach*, she's quiet enough.' I didn't say anything, she was certainly putting on a good show.

We climbed back into the van and headed for home but I could not help looking back as we drove out of the yard, just to see if the sow was still behaving herself. The wretched animal was actually walking straight into a pen and not a cross word spoken. Nevertheless, I did wonder if we would have a repeat screeching contest when we went to collect her. Malcolm must have read my thoughts. 'I know how I'll anchor that partition down to stop the old devil,' he mused. I did not bother to ask for the technical details, just the assurance that the retaining partition would retain. Whatever Malcolm did must have worked, for when the sow was collected two days later, the whole operation went off quite smoothly. We repeated the exercise the following week with the Landrace sow and no problems.

I began to think that we had at last got the measure of our mini herd of swine, but life is full of surprises, as I would have the pleasure of finding out. Apparently, we would have to wait four months before the birth of the litters. During that time we increased our swine herd by forty as we bought in from market another four sows and their litters of two eights and two tens. These sows were Welsh crossed either with Large White or Landrace. This cross produced good strong pigs that were not so inclined to put on as much fat as the Large White and not as long in the body as the Landrace, which had a tendency to weakness in the back legs. If we were lucky enough to find a Welsh cross with one or more black spots, so much the better, this being the sign of a Wessex Saddleback somewhere in its ancestry, again a healthy breed.

Feeding our livestock was quite a simple routine. The sows that had litters were kept and fed in the sties, as were those pigs that had been weaned and were now being fattened for pork or bacon – depending on their growth-rate and shape. Sows that were 'in pig' were allowed to road the three bottom fields and would come up to the house and feed from a trough.

Like all creatures, they knew when it was time for food and could always be seen at the appropriate time, hanging around the troughs waiting for their barley meal. If by any chance they were not near the trough, a shake of the bucket handle and a loud 'Hoy! Hoy!' would soon bring them racing up to the house, ears flapping up and down like a herd of African elephants and the same colour as well, if they had been rolling in the mud.

We had placed two troughs together to make a long feeding line and had staked them firmly into the ground to stop the sows turning the troughs over before they had completely finished their meal of whey and barley.

It was one evening whilst we were watching the sows sucking whey noisily through their teeth that Malcolm voiced the opinion that we ought to put rings in their noses to stop them tearing up the ground. I must say they certainly made a good job of it, so much so that if they could be trained to forage in straight lines, mechanical ploughing would be quite unnecessary.

'I think I'll fix fencing bars along the length of the trough and make divisions just wide enough and long enough for each sow to be able to feed individually. Also, when we want to catch them we would only have to creep up behind them with a piece of tin and they would be contained within the feeding partition,' said Malcolm. It certainly sounded better than our previous attempts at trying to catch a sow. They became very wily after they have been allowed to roam free in the fields, which meant a lot of extra craft on our part was needed to capture them.

One of the sows that we had taken to the boar for service came 'on hogging' – which meant that she was not pregnant when she should have been. This happens three weeks after an unsuccessful service, in which case the sow is taken back to the boar for another session. We spent three quarters of an hour cavorting round the fields with pieces of corrugated zinc, trying to corner the creature so that we could guide her into the sty ready to be loaded into the Bradford. In the end we had to leave a food trail of pellets leading into one of the pens and wait patiently whilst the greedy animal sucked up every single piece. This was successful but very exasperating, to say the least. Consequently, we were ready to try any method that might be a little easier and less time-consuming.

'If I put the bars in position this evening and give the sows a couple of days to get used to them, we could try catching the blighters for ringing on Saturday,' suggested Malcolm.

Malcolm spent the next couple of hours sawing and hammering, and gradually our pig catching equipment took shape. The next morning, at feeding time, we filled the troughs as usual then stood back to watch. The sows came to within three feet of our trap and eyed it very suspiciously, wanting to feed but obviously feeling that something was not quite right.

Eventually, the Large White sow decided that she was not going to miss her breakfast and very, very slowly started to walk into one of the partitions. She was halfway in when she realised that she was being channelled to the trough; she moved smartly into reverse and backed into the other sows that had edged in behind her. Pandemonium broke out, with sows jumping about in all directions. However they gradually quietened down when again the Large White decided to have another try – after all, nothing had actually happened to her, had it?

She cautiously made her way to the trough, concluded all was well and started to eat noisily. This was obviously too much for the sows who had been watching from a safe distance, for they immediately threw all caution to the wind and shot into the divisions to join their friends at breakfast. 'That's great,' whooped Malcolm, 'they'll be in there like a flash this evening, you see.' And they were. Saturday arrived. Time to put our sow catching campaign into action. Malcolm had decided that the partition would probably not be strong enough to withstand a sow being roped to it, so the plan was that he would stand on top of the rails above the trough, holding a huge rope noose, the bottom of which lay camouflaged on the ground. The idea being that as soon as the sow went to the trough and had her two front legs over the noose, Malcolm would pull up the rope which would tighten the noose round the sow's stomach. He was then going to try to guide her towards the old oak tree which grew halfway down the field, some sixty yards away, and tie her to that so that the ringing operation could be carried out, a feat which took place quicker than we had anticipated.

It was the Large White sow Lantern Jaw that approached the trough, now filled with tempting barley meal. She did not appear to notice Malcolm or the noose that he was holding from above, for she walked straight over the base of the loop which was on the ground. As soon as her body was halfway through, Malcolm pulled hard on the rope, which immediately tightened around the body of the sow. As soon as she felt the rope around her bulging stomach, she backed out of the partition and took off at about twenty miles an hour, pulling Malcolm straight off his perch into the mud. Luckily, he did not let go of the rope, but he did not have time to stand still either.

The sow went galloping down the field with Malcolm hanging on some fifteen feet behind, his face covered in mud, yelling like a demon from an African jungle – the translation of which meant that I was to try and head off the sow preventing her from running too far below the oak tree. A fat chance I had of doing that. Wearing a pair of Malcolm's old Wellington boots, I could hardly put one leg in front of the other, let alone break the world record for the sixty-yard dash. However Malcolm, not to be daunted, made for the left side of the oak tree whilst the sow went to the right. They arrived together. Malcolm pulled hard on his end and ran twice round the tree and the sow. A perfect anchor was formed and the two of them ended up with three feet of rope between them.

Still puffing like the runaway train, Malcolm shouted

to me with instructions to bring the fine rope and pig-ringing tool that he had left by the trough. And hurry. I clumped over the field as quickly as my seven league boots would allow, dutifully carrying the necessary equipment.

'Right, now hang onto this rope whilst I put the finer rope into her mouth behind her tusks and tighten a noose over her nose.' I hung onto the rope and sow as if my life depended on it; Malcolm quickly fitted the finer rope and instructed me to let go of the main noose but to keep constant pressure on the smaller noose. With the sow and myself pulling in opposite directions we managed to stay in the same place. This enabled Malcolm to slip the ring through the sow's nose – actually he put in two rings. Strangely enough, although the pig squealed the whole time that I was hanging onto the rope, there was no difference in tone at all when the rings went into her gristly snout.

The job was done; a quick jerk on the rope released the knot and the sow was free again. What a performance. We certainly had a good laugh about it, but decided that there must be easier ways of ringing pigs. We were certainly learning by experience – though I was coming to the conclusion that my beloved preferred a difficult job to an easy one and secretly enjoyed thinking up crazy ways of performing them.

Chapter Four

One of the steers we had bought – the Hereford cross Shorthorn – had suddenly taken it into its head that it should be allowed to roam freely, like his bison brothers in North America, and that the whole of the Welsh countryside was his for the munching. He would find a weak spot in the hedge, and if there wasn't one then he would make one by just sticking his head through the greenery and pushing his eight hundredweight frame hard against it until he was through, and of course the other four steers followed. He would only have a few mouthfuls of grass and move on to the next hedge and repeat the performance. It did not seem to matter whether he broke into lush pasture or a barren rush-and-thistle field, the objective was to break out. Unfortunately, apart from damaging the hedges, he and his friends were flattening grass that was almost ready to be cut for hay. Our neighbours had been very good and not complained at all but obviously we would quickly have to find a way of stopping our four-legged Houdini.

'I remember we had a cow like that at home,' said Malcolm one evening after we had driven the cattle back into our own fields and mended yet two more holes. 'I seem to remember my father tied a stake across her horns; I suppose it would have the effect of making the animal think she was wider than she was and therefore would not be able to penetrate the hole she was trying to make in the hedge. Anyway, it would be worth a try.'

The cattle were in the sloping field above the house, moving gently across the grass, curling their tongues round the lush green spears and chasing it over their ever-grinding teeth. They looked docile enough, but I bet their leader was quietly eyeing the hedge, searching for the next escape hole.

'We'll ease them into the top corner of the field. I'll grab the horns of our escapologist, give them a quick jerk, and he'll be on the ground quite helpless. You can then tie the stake onto the horns with this binder twine,' said Malcolm, handing me a length of orange string.

'That sounds quite dangerous to me,' I ventured. I had seen this done in cowboy films with young calves, but would my dear husband really be able to throw a two-year-old steer? Malcolm must have seen the doubtful look in my eye.

'I used to do it with calves on the farm at home; the principle is the same, it's just that the animal is a bit bigger. So I don't see why it shouldn't work,' he finished almost defiantly.

So we gradually edged the cattle towards the top corner of the field. We had them contained almost in a funnel, fifteen feet wide and about twenty feet deep. They stood quite still, eyeing us very suspiciously as we faced them, our arms outstretched trying to form a barrier.

'Right,' whispered Malcolm, 'you stay still and I'll walk very slowly towards them.' Houdini was in the middle of the group and watched almost mesmerised as Malcolm approached them. Suddenly, Malcolm seemed to leap the last three feet, grabbed the creature by the horns, gave the necessary flick and the steer was on the ground. But so was Malcolm. They were locked in combat, slithering and rolling down the slope – the steer trying hard to slacken Malcolm's grip and he equally determined to hang on to those horns. It seemed an eternity before they eventually parted company, with Houdini the winner. Malcolm was just no match for nearly one thousand pounds of beef.

'No matter,' grinned Malcolm, ruefully rubbing his knees, elbows and rear, 'we'll have him yet. We'll drive them into the old pigsty by the road.'

Malcolm was full of bright ideas today. So, we trudged down the hill to the old traditional type of sty – a six feet square courtyard which stood proud of a dark, low-entranced, very basic stone shed.

'But we'll never get them in there,' I wailed, envisaging yet another impossible task. My pioneering spirit was not very high today.

'Yes, we will,' my husband assured me. 'Should have put them in there in the first place really.'

Meanwhile, our marauding herd had kicked up its heels, galloped through the gate at the bottom of the field and were now in the lower field, swishing their tails, ears pricked and looking at each other as if to say, 'I wonder what their next trick will be.' Well, they would not have long to find out. Malcolm swung open the heavy gate that breached the front of the pigsty in readiness, we hoped, for the cattle. He then joined me well below the watching group of animals. We did not hurry them, just gently guided them towards the house. We badgered them as far as the yard and it was obvious that at most we would only be able to contain three steers into the confines of the stone sty. Fortunately, Houdini was leading the escapees, so if we were lucky enough and I was clever enough to head off the steers we did not want, and Malcolm was swift enough slamming the heavy gate quickly behind, we would have our trio trapped in the sty. It worked. The front three steers were in the pen before they realised there was no way out; even so, Houdini managed to turn round and was facing Malcolm as he drove home the bolt on the gate. They were imprisoned in the sty, packed like the proverbial sardines, head to tail.

In my innocence, I thought that it would be an easy task to tie on the wooden stake, but no. Malcolm tried to attach the stake by standing on the bars of the gate, leaning across the first steer at an angle of eighty-nine degrees to wrestle with the horns of Houdini, who was jammed tightly in the middle of the group. Each time Malcolm just touched the horns of the wretched animal it would toss its head from side to side faster than any Wimbledon spectator.

'It's no good, we'll have to hold his head,' said Malcolm. Five months pregnant, my stomach turned over; what he meant was, I, June Baker would have to hold the animal's head. I was learning this double talk language fast.

'All you have to do,' soothed my dear husband, 'is to stand in the pen close to Houdini's shoulder (I would have no option on the closeness bit, there wasn't room to do anything else), put your thumb in one nostril and your index finger in the other one and pinch them together. Hard. At the same time, pull the head to one side and back and you'll find that he just will not move.'

'What if he stamps all over my feet?' I did not want to have to have shoes made to fit over two circular feet, they were big enough already and I was quite keen to keep them the traditional shape. Imagine trying to ski with feet like steak plates – still, perhaps I wouldn't need skis if that were the case.

'Come on,' Malcolm interrupted my thoughts,

'squeeze in between Houdini and the steer near the gate and pull his nose towards me, then I'll be able to reach the horns easier.'

I climbed very slowly over the gate, took a deep breath and edged myself nervously between the two steers. I was halfway along the side of Houdini and decided that I would try to bring his head round from there. I thought I might get kicked but I would not get stamped on, though I still couldn't quite make up my mind which would be the worst option. I reached attentively for his nose, but, as soon as he felt my hands touch him, he started tossing his head again from side to side.

'That's no good at all,' commented my leader, from the safe side of the gate. 'Get right up by his head, lean right into his side, pinch his nose really hard and pull his head firmly round towards his shoulder.'

'It's all right for you to give the order,' I grumbled. 'There's hardly room to breathe in here.' Still, I'd show them, Malcolm and that wretched cow or steer or whatever it was.

I eased forward, up to the steer's shoulder and started to push my weight against Houdini – whereupon he promptly started pushing back.

'He's pushing me,' I quavered.

'Well, push him back and grab hold of his nose.'

'Right, I jolly well will,' I shouted, getting more and more cross with each second.

I leaned so hard into Houdini's side that he had to take a step to steady himself. I pinched into his nostrils so hard that my finger and thumb almost met; then I pulled his nose firmly towards his side. Success.

I could hardly believe it. I looked up at Malcolm who was grinning from ear to ear.

'See,' he said, 'I knew you could do it.'

'Just you stop your grinning and fix that stake to this animal's head. I'm not in here for my health you know,' I scowled.

Houdini was breathing very hard on my hand and his eyes looked far too big for their sockets; anyone would think that I was trying to strangle him. When I thought about it, I probably was. What if he started to really struggle?

My bravado was running out fast.

'Hurry up, Malcolm,' it was my turn to do some cajoling. 'My fingers ache.' What a daft excuse – but I couldn't get out of that pen quick enough.

That was a point; what was going to happen when I released that steaming nose?

'Hey Malcolm, how do I escape from here without being crushed or have my eyes poked out by that stake which you have at last managed to tie on to Houdini's horns?'

We did not have long to wait. We stood hidden behind a hedge and watched Houdini, who obviously thought that he had to show the other steers that he was still in command. He gradually munched his way towards the boundary hedge, selected what he thought was a weak spot and started to push, but the stake which protruded six inches either side of his large, bony head, lodged against the stronger branches and stopped him completely.

Somewhat baffled, he withdrew his head from the shaking greenery, walked about five yards further down and tried again. Once more he was unsuccessful.

After a third attempt he decided to give in gracefully, for he turned his back on the hedge, surveyed the other steers with a very supercilious air and walked sedately down to the stream, wearing his stake like the crown of a highland stag.

We left the stake on Houdini's head for two weeks and thankfully, he never attempted to break out again, much to our relief and that of our long suffering neighbours.

Despite the Houdini cow episode, my pregnancy managed to go full term and we were fortunate to produce Shelly – a strong-willed sister for Leigh – three months later.

Chapter Five

Fishing was a sport that had never really interested me; the idea of sitting on a riverbank dangling a wriggling worm in the water for hours on end just did not appeal. I had never actually seen anyone catch a fish, although I had watched many hopeful fishermen on river bank, canal slope and quarry pit. Even those who fished from sea walls and piers seemed to fare no better. I really believed it was just an excuse to sit down and do nothing for a few hours and that the fishing rods, twisting worms, heaving white maggots and rotten fish (that must have been purchased from the local fish shop at least ten days earlier) were all a guise to hide tired eyes or a crafty move to dodge digging the garden.

So, you can imagine why, when Malcolm suggested one fine July evening that we might try to catch a few trout in our little stream, I didn't immediately race out into the garden and start frantically digging for worms. Equally, I was a little puzzled; Malcolm had never shown an interest in fishing before and he was not one for sitting down for more than ten minutes at a time. So, why the sudden urge to fish?

'We haven't any rods, have we?' I queried.

'Oh, we'll just take a quiet walk and look, then we'll see about the fishing bit later.' Well, that didn't sound too bad, a stroll along the banks of our little stream was always a very pleasant way of passing a free hour. We wandered down to the bottom field and made for the gaunt twisted tree that had once been struck by lightning, where often a heron would stand, watching the water for hours – looking like one of the silvered branches of the stricken tree, the blue flash above his eye being the only colour against the soft greys.

He wasn't there this evening, and even if he had been he would have soon taken off at our approach, but even then he would have left it until the last possible second, hoping that he blended in so well with his background that we would not notice him. Then we would hear the heavy, laborious downward beat of the huge wings, just managing lift off, trailing his large feet like the floats of a sea plane, drifting across the field only inches above the ground, until he landed feet first a safe distance from his intruders, once more to merge into the surroundings. Beautiful birds, always solitary, almost prehistoric.

I followed Malcolm stealthily along the bank, pausing every now and then to look into the gentle flowing stream that meandered like unpicked knitting wool along the boundary of our lowest field, forming numerous perfect oxbows as it rippled softly along. Malcolm always spotted a trout before I did. Sometimes they hid in the shadows of trailing willow fronds that hung from the banks, mutely caressing the little brook; or in the safety of an overhang, their little noses just showing in the light of the main stream. Others swam brazenly in mid stream, waving their tails in time with the tawny water weed that gave them such perfect camouflage.

After a quarter of an hour of peaceful trout studying, I ventured to ask how Malcolm intended to catch our fishy friends. His answer was not the answer I expected, or would any self-respecting fisherman.

'With a spade,' he replied.

'A spade?' I exclaimed. 'What on earth do you mean?'

A chuckle was the immediate reply. Malcolm then proceeded to initiate the uninitiated.

'It's quite simple; we just dig across one of these oxbows, diverting the water straight through to the main stream, and the trout that are left behind in the pool will be ours.' I'm afraid that it did not occur to me that this was wrong in any way; in fact, I didn't even think it would work, but it would be an interesting experiment.

'First we need a spade,' declared Malcolm.

No points for guessing who had the honour of walking back to the house to fetch the spade and who had the job of selecting the right place to dig.

I puffed back to the stream some ten minutes later, dutifully humping the trenching spade, only to find my beloved reclining against a willow tree, eyes half closed, puffing lazily on his favourite pipe. He must have noticed my red face and my best impersonation of the Royal Scot steam engine as I huffed to a halt, for he quickly patted the ground beside him and said, as I had been so quick, I had better sit down and get my breath back and watch him work for five minutes. I flopped onto the dampening grass and watched the last of the smoke from Malcolm's pipe rise slowly into the still evening air. It really was a beautiful spot. The willow dipped its lower branches into the stream, the water running through the leaves as if cooling the elegant green fingers.

I was beginning to appreciate the fisherman's logic – the relaxing, looking and seeing all things that moved; the fish, if you caught any, was a bonus. But there was a snag. As we were not fishing in the orthodox manner I was not to have the benefit of the normal long 'sit' allocated to normal fishermen.

The spot Malcolm had chosen for our diversion necessitated digging a narrow, four-feet-long channel. This did not take very long as the ground was quite soft. As we neared the last six inches, I found that I was becoming quite excited. I wondered how fast the water would rush through the narrow ditch. Would all the fish be dragged through with the sudden surge of the course change?

'Right,' said Malcolm with the spade poised above the last cut. 'Let's break the dam gates.'

The water raced through the narrow opening, leaping and jostling its way to the main stream. Within minutes the new stretch of the stream had settled down to the same gentle, flowing rhythm as its parent, but the bow that we had isolated looked forlorn and dead with the life of the stream taken away. There was no sign at all of any fish; perhaps the 'Fish Diversion' idea wasn't going to work after all.

'Come on,' Malcolm broke into my doubting thoughts, 'we'll go back to the house now and come back in the morning.'

I made no comment but I certainly had plenty of doubtful thoughts about my husband's fishing technique.

Our young son usually managed to wake us by six o'clock each morning and this day was no exception. It did not take long to satisfy his hungry shouts and we were soon able to don Wellingtons and track through the dew-drenched grass in the early morning sun and down to the stream.

Again that feeling of excitement; would there be any fish? If there were, how many would there be? How big? How small? Thank goodness we did not have far to go. We pushed aside the willow fronds and there in the marooned oxbow gleamed several shafts of silver. Eleven slippery trout was the catch of the day, which we gathered with some delight, but I think we both felt that we would not fish that way again.

Chapter Six

My first encounter with bees happened when I was working for a firm of estate agents in Carmarthen, not long after we were married. A client was in the process of buying a cottage but had discovered that a swarm of bees had taken over the attic and were busily ensconced in their daily business of making honey. Unfortunately, the would-be purchaser did not like honey and liked bees even less, and certainly did not want them as such close neighbours, and refused to sign the completion contract until she was given a guarantee that the bees were no longer in residence.

The agent who was dealing with the matter had dictated a letter to me, which was to be sent to the local beekeepers' association, asking them if they would remove the bees for the normal fee of £5. I knew that Malcolm was interested in keeping bees as he had told me that he had often watched and helped his mother with them when he was a child. So I asked Bob, the agent, if perhaps we would hold the letter for a couple of days and let Malcolm have the opportunity of clearing the bees. Bob did not seem to think a couple of days would make much difference, and needless to say Malcolm was delighted with the idea and possibility of becoming a beekeeper.

'Hopefully we shall acquire a swarm of bees and get paid £5 for doing it,' he chuckled.

'But don't forget,' warned Bob, 'every single bee and

every trace of honey is to be removed. How you do it is your business, but the best of luck.' The way Bob added that last phrase certainly gave the impression that he was glad that he was not in charge of moving the bees.

That evening we drove out to Brechfa to find the cottage and study the problem of removing the bees with benefit to both us and them. We found the little cottage, not unlike our own with the basic two rooms up and two rooms down, and like ours it must have been empty for years. It was tucked right on the edge of the forest, the trees towering over the peeling whitewashed walls, the garden an absolute wilderness. Although it was an early evening in June, the high thick hedge and many trees made the cottage very dark and gloomy. We opened the blistered, brown painted door (how I used to love popping paint blisters on my grandfather's sheds when I was a child, it doesn't seem to happen these days) and stood in the dark hall, our eyes taking several seconds to adjust to the dark interior. It took very little time to look at the two rooms downstairs or the two rooms upstairs. But it took a little longer to find the very small trap door in the ceiling of the slightly larger bedroom, which obviously opened into the roof space.

'That's lucky,' said Malcolm. 'So many of these old cottages do not have access into the roof space, which means that you have to remove some of the tiles and climb in via the roof.'

Under the trap door stood a rickety old chair which looked as if it had been the main food supply for decades of woodworm beetles and had obviously been put there by possible buyers to spy on the bees.

'Right, let's go and have a look and see what problems we're going to have,' said my intrepid hero, balancing very precariously on the worm-eaten chair.

'You'll never get through that little hole; you'll get stuck,' I gasped as Malcolm struggled to push his shoulders through the tiny square. With much huffing and puffing and heaving, he eventually hauled his six feet and two inches of body into the roof space.

'Pass me the torch please; I can't see a thing.'

I stepped gingerly onto the chair and passed the torch up to Malcolm and stuck my head through the hole just as Malcolm switched on the beam of light. He swung the torch up and down the length of the roof fairly quickly and at first sight it seemed that the attic was quite empty; then a slight movement in one corner drew the beam for a closer inspection. A colony of about sixty bats had moved in and taken 'upside down' residence between the rafters. Some just hung motionless, gripping the timbers with their tiny, sharp claws; others turned their heads from side to side as if chatting to each other – there was certainly a lot of squeaking coming from that direction.

Every now and then one of them would decide to fly to the end of the attic and back, gliding swiftly and silently between the beams with never a falter. What amazing little creatures they are. Malcolm was now shining the torch on the opposite corner and muttering to himself, 'Fantastic; how clever, incredible.' What could he see that I could not?

'Hey,' I shouted, still balancing on the chair, 'are there any bees and are they dangerous?'

'Well,' said Malcolm, 'it was the bees; it's perfectly safe now. Come and have a look.'

With not quite so much heaving and tugging, I was hauled through the very small trap door and found myself swaying on the cross timbers. I stepped very carefully from one beam to the next with a terrible urge to step on the lathe and plaster in between the beams – but, eventually, made it to the corner. Delicate parchment-coloured honeycomb hung in curtains from the sloping roof.

Each sheet of comb must have been a yard long and two and a half feet wide, and there were fifteen of them. A great pile of dead bees lay at the base of the comb curtain.

'What a feat,' I said in awe, 'they must have been here for years.' To think that insects can make such a construction – each hexagon perfectly made with exact precision.

'They must have started in the corner and gradually worked their way out,' said Malcolm. 'The comb there is much darker in colour. Look, you can see the old brood cells here at the bottom; this end is definitely more recent.' He gave the appropriate end a smart tap – a deep resonant hum filled the air.

'Goodness, they're still alive,' gasped Malcolm.

'Alive,' I echoed. I raced across the roof timbers as sure-footed as any mountain goat, dropped through the hatch onto the rickety chair and would have been out through the garden gate in one minute flat if Malcolm had not called me back.

'Look,' he said, his face appearing in the hole in the ceiling, 'there's no need for alarm.'

'But those bees are alive,' I interrupted, 'and you've always told me never to swat or hit bees or they get cross; well, you've just thumped their honey mine and they didn't sound too pleased about it, did they?' I finished.

'Well,' said Malcolm in a very patient voice; 'it's true, they did hum a bit when I tapped the comb, but they didn't fly at us, did they?'

'No. And they're not going to get the chance to either as far as I'm concerned.'

'I think they must be right at the base of the comb, but near the wall,' Malcolm continued, completely ignoring my outburst. 'You needn't come back up; I'll just have a closer look to see exactly the best way to remove them.'

Malcolm turned away from the hatch whilst I stayed in the gloomy bedroom, wondering if I should be brave and go back into the attic but, within three minutes, he was easing himself down through the ceiling hatch but not in such a hurry as I expected.

'They are right at the base and a very strong swarm, but I don't know whether we'll be lucky enough to find the queen and collect a large enough nucleus of bees to form a new colony.'

The big question was, how were we going to remove the bees but still have them healthy enough to set up shop in our own hive? Smoking them, the traditional way of handling bees, was of no use. It would be too large an area to control. Even if we did not want to have them to keep for ourselves, one would not be able to just hack away all the bees and comb without causing a massive disturbance, to say the least.

'Pity we can't dope the lot of them,' I laughed.

'That could well be the answer,' replied Malcolm. 'If we could get hold of some chloroform, soak a rag with it and put it underneath them, hopefully it would make them dozy enough to handle. We could find the queen, put a load of bees with her into a box, shovel all the comb into a couple of sacks and the job would be done.'

'And just where do you think we're going to get any chloroform from?' I asked. 'You can't buy it over the counter like cough mixture, you know.'

'I know that – but if you went into a chemist and told them exactly what you wanted it for, I'm sure they would let you have some,' Malcolm countered.

'They'd probably cart me off to St David's (the local mental hospital) and lock me up, or telephone the police. Anyway, why me? Why can't you go and ask for some?'

''Cause you're so much better at that sort of thing than I am.'

'Flattery will get you nowhere, Malcolm B.' But it did.

During my lunch hour the next day I went into one of the chemists in the town and asked the young sales assistant if she could let me have some chloroform. She gave me a most peculiar look, she told me not to go away and she would ask the chief chemist, as it was a rather unusual request. She seemed to be gone for absolutely ages. Perhaps they thought I had some antisocial ideas in mind, like killing someone, and they had telephoned the police. I was beginning to think I might do myself some good if I left the shop rather smartly when the assistant suddenly appeared with – presumably – the chief chemist. He was a short, fat, balding man – rather like a middle-aged Billy Bunter; a pair of spectacles perched on the end of his nose, though he did not seem to use them, as he constantly peered over the top of them.

'Well young lady, for what reason do you require chloroform?' The words were accompanied with a very hard, penetrating stare.

'Um... Well... You see, it's for some bees,' I stammered.

'Oh yes,' says he – obviously thinking that the best tactic was to humour me.

'Yes, you see there's this cottage up in the woods near Brechfa with a huge swarm of bees in the roof and we, that's my husband and I, thought that if we could chloroform them, they'd be dopey enough for us to be able to find the queen and, more to the point, they wouldn't be flying around all over the place, we'd stand a better chance of not getting badly stung and we would be able to remove them more easily from the roof space,' I blurted out breathlessly.

The chemist started to chuckle.

'I've never heard such a daft idea, but it might just work.' He disappeared into his room at the back of the shop and two minutes later reappeared with a small bottle of colourless liquid.

'There you are, my dear, there's enough chloroform there to put paid to two men, but seriously, you must be very careful; once you've tipped it out of the bottle, you must stand well clear. Let me know how you get on with your bee catching, I'll be most interested in the results,' he said as he retreated into his dispensary.

I paid the assistant two shillings and six pence for the lethal dose and scuttled gleefully out of the shop; I did not even sign a book for the chloroform.

Malcolm arrived at five o'clock to pick me up from the office. I hardly had time to scrabble into the car before he asked if I had managed to buy the 'bee medicine'. I told him exactly what had happened and that I felt as if I was involved in some dastardly plot.

'And so you are,' he laughed as we drove away.

During the day Malcolm had told Mr Finch (the factory manager who was a very ardent bee-keeper) about the bees in the roof of the little cottage.

Always keen to start someone on the honey trail, he seemed to be more than delighted to offer us the use of a hive and veil; we were now on our way to pick up these two vital pieces of equipment. Mr Finch had arrived at his home just before us and had already put the veil to one side.

'You had better try the veil on,' he said to Malcolm, 'and I'll show you how to make sure that it's pulled down properly over the shoulders for complete protection.'

He handed Malcolm a straw hat with a wide brim and a pointed dome; a black muslin veil hung from the brim which could be tightened with a cord which ran through the base of the veil. Malcolm put on the veil, looking like a cross between David Livingstone and a boy scout. Mr Finch pulled the black netting over Malcolm's shoulders and clear of his neck, pulling the collar on Malcolm's shirt well up thus keeping the net away from the back of his neck should the bees try to burrow into any of the gathered netting. The spare hive that Mr Finch was going to let us borrow, stood in his conservatory – it took only a couple of minutes to load it into the back of the Bradford, next to a pile of sacks that Malcolm had acquired, and a cardboard box.

'What's in the box?' I enquired.

'Oh, I bought a camping lantern together with a gas bottle. It will give a much better light than the torch and it'll always come in useful anyway,' said Malcolm.

'Well, the best of luck,' said Mr Finch, 'I hope you manage to get the bees out alive, but I have my doubts. Roof bees are always very difficult to take and to keep going. Still, you never know.' He slapped the side of the van and we were on our way. Well, almost. We had decided to go back to our flat, set up the hive ready for the bees and have some tea before embarking on our bee catching expedition in Brechfa. We parked by the back gate then carried the empty hive across the small orchard and set it down under the hedge the front of it apparently facing east.

'That,' said Malcolm in reply to my obvious question, 'is so that the bees catch the first rays of the sun in the morning.'

'Why, would they oversleep if we faced them to the west?' I laughed.

'Laugh if you must, but if we're going to keep bees, we may as well do it properly.' Detecting a distinct tone of disapproval, I decided that I had better keep my giggles to myself.

We stood the four legs of the hive on house bricks; this was to give the hive a little height and better ventilation, but mainly to prevent the legs from sinking into the ground and rotting, and also to keep the hive on an even keel. We had some tea then once again headed in the direction of Brechfa.

On arrival at the cottage we relieved the Bradford of its bee catching equipment and humped it upstairs as far as the rickety chair. Once more Malcolm eased himself through the hole in the ceiling; then he was asking for the lantern to be passed up, with the instruction that I should light the lantern, as there would then be more light for me to see what I was doing than if he lit the lantern in the attic. A simple operation, you would think.

'First lift the glass sleeve which protects the mantle; strike a match and hold the flame close to the mantle and turn the screw forward to the "plus" position.' Thus came the instructions from above.

So... I lifted the glass, struck the match and tried to turn the screw, but nothing happened except that I burnt my fingers as the flame reached the end of the match.

'Try and turn the screw first to loosen it up a bit; it's

probably a little stiff because it's new,' said the heavenly voice. Eventually, I was able to turn the screw forward and back fairly easily.

'Now,' said Malcolm, 'try again.' I did. I lifted the glass, struck the match, turned on the gas, and the glass sleeve slipped in my hand and dropped down and put out the flame on the match.

'And again' came the voice – this time slightly exasperated, I thought. This time, success – the mantle glowed into life.

'Don't turn the gas on too full too soon or you'll crack the glass,' called my overseer from above. What a performance. I passed the lighted lantern up to Malcolm with half a smirk on my face.

'I don't know what you're grinning about,' he growled.

'Well I did light it eventually, didn't I?' I said, smiling sweetly.

The light disappeared into the black hole. A couple of seconds later Malcolm's head appeared, silhouetted against the glow of the lantern.

'If you would like to pass up the spade, sacks, chloroform, sheeting and my old gloves, I'll get to work.' I passed the necessary items up through the twenty-inch square hole.

'I think I had better put the veil on just in case those bees decide to get too lively,' said Malcolm.

'Do you think they'll come down here?' I queried from my rickety chair.

'No. You'll be all right down there. It's pretty dark and bees don't normally like flying in the dark anyway.' I must say I was relieved to hear that Malcolm put on the wide-brimmed straw hat and let the black netting fall on to his shoulders; he then tightened the cord and tucked the veil under the lapels and collar of his jacket. I noticed that the bats were still playing tag the full length of the roof space.

I watched from my precarious perch as Malcolm spread the sheet under the comb. He then soaked a piece of cloth with the chloroform and pushed it under the honeycomb at the point where he thought the bees were most active. It was not long before he was back at the hatch.

'If the bees don't soon go to sleep, I certainly will. The fumes are certainly wafting about.' Rather than climb back down the hatch, Malcolm dropped on all fours and stuck his head down the hole, breathing the somewhat fresher air from the bedroom. After about ten minutes he decided to make an inspection to see if the bees were at all sleepy. The bats were certainly quiet and no longer zoomed up and down the attic at fifty miles an hour. Again I watched from the opening, fingers gripping the sides of the hatch, eyes and nose just level with the ceiling joists. Malcolm tapped the side of the honey-comb; a number of bees dropped onto the outspread sheet and started to crawl all over each other. An equal number of bees flew up out of the comb and either made for Malcolm or the light. Thank goodness he had the veil tied on securely.

'They seem to be quite dozy, but not as quiet as I had hoped,' said Malcolm. 'Whatever happens they must be moved out of the roof, so I may as well get on with it.'

Malcolm started breaking the comb away from the roof and the wall, starting at the end and working inwards. After about five minutes, but what seemed more like five hours, he turned and called out that he could not find the queen.

'I think I'll just have to shovel the whole lot into the sacks and they'll just have to sort themselves into some sort of order if they possibly can.'

With that Malcolm picked up the spade and hacked out large segments of comb and bees, scooping the mixture into one of the sacks. He tied the top with string in what I hoped was a very strong knot. I noticed that there were about thirty bees crawling about on the outside of the bundle; Malcolm did not seem at all worried about them. He picked up the bulging sack and started to walk somewhat unsteadily across the roof timbers towards the hatch. I was off the chair, down the stairs and had reached the front door before I heard him shouting, 'Hey! Where are you?'

'I'm down by the front door,' I shouted back.

'Well, come back here and take these bees from me.'

'But they're crawling about all over the outside of the sack,' I yelled.

'Oh, don't be so daft,' came the exasperated reply. 'They won't hurt you.'

'What have they got stingers for then?' I called from the bottom of the stairs.

'Come on,' he cajoled. 'I promise you won't get stung.'

'You might keep your promise but will the bees back you up?' I had reluctantly returned to the top of the stairs. 'But I haven't got a veil,' I wailed, knowing full well by now that I would have to take the bulging bundle from Malcolm. I stood by the bedroom door.

'Look,' said Malcolm, 'I'll pass them down through the hatch; you stand on the chair but to one side and you will be able to take them from me quite safely.'

I had no time for more protests. The sack was already

being lowered through the ceiling, bees on the inside, bees on the outside, and all buzzing the same crazy tune. 'A fat lot of good that chloroform was,' I moaned.

'They'd be singing a lot louder than that if we had not had the chloroform,' said Malcolm.

I looked up at Malcolm's face, obscured by the veil but I was well able to see about twenty odd bees crawling all over his hat and shoulders. I took a deep breath and grabbed hold of the swaying sack and hoped that the chair would not break with the extra weight.

'What shall I do with it?' I shouted.

'Put it on the ground at the back of the van and I'll sort it out when I come down; then come back up here and I'll have the next lot ready for you.'

'Thanks very much. How lucky can one get?' I asked. I negotiated the steep stairs with some difficulty. Although I held the sack at arm's length, when I bent my knees to go down a step, the sack brushed against my knees. I eventually reached the bottom but I still had to carry the bees down the path to the van. It was then I felt the tickling on the back of my hand. A bee had crawled off the sack onto my clenched hand and was now crawling gently up my arm. As I looked down I caught sight of another hanging on the end of my hair; they must have fallen off Malcolm when he handed the bees to me from the hatch. Terrified that the fresh air might revive any others that might be hanging on the sack, I galloped down the path as if all the devils in hell were at my heels. I was in a state of collapse by the time I reached the van. I set the sticky haul (as by this time honey was beginning to ooze gently through the sacking) none too gently on the ground, flicked the bee out of my hair, the other off my arm, and searched for any others that might be hiding on my clothes. I could not find any but I felt as if they were crawling all over me. I shuddered from head to toe. Still, it was no use thinking that was the end of it; I knew that I had to go back into the cottage and help Malcolm with the rest of the bees. I climbed back up the stairs just in time to see another sack being lowered through the ceiling. It was just too much, I burst into laughter; tears rolled down my face as I laughed and cried at the same time.

'What on earth's the matter? Are you all right?' called Malcolm.

'Yes, fine,' I answered, though the strain was beginning to tell.

'I was just wondering who was looniest of the two of us; you up there with bees crawling all over you or me down here daft enough to take great sacks of the blighters from you.'

'Come on, stop larking about and we'll soon be finished.'

'I would have finished half an hour ago if I had had my way,' I replied. Malcolm ignored my comments as he let go of the sack.

'Not so many bees in that sack,' he said. 'I should think another two sackfuls should see us somewhere near finished.'

Twice more I made the trip down the stairs and along the path – both times with no escapees. Back then up the stairs, hopefully for the last time. I stood on the chair and peered into the attic. The bats were beginning to stir – the effects of the chloroform certainly did not last very long. Malcolm had really made a very good job of clearing away the honeycomb, so that part of the job was successful. We would at least have earned the five pounds for clearing the roof space and possibly gained some good active bees to produce honey for us. One last sack was threaded through the ceiling; it certainly was a tight fit. I dumped it next to the other three and returned once more to my rickety chair to take the spade, lantern and sheeting from Malcolm's outstretched hand before he eased himself once more through the ceiling hatch.

'Come on, let's get outside and you can de-bee me,' he said.

Out into the garden and fresh air – what bliss. There were just four bees on the outside of the veil and three on his jacket.

'Lucky you had the veil on,' I said, flicking the bees well away from us into the dusk.

'You're absolutely right. Even then two of them managed to get inside so there must be a small hole in the netting somewhere.'

'Did they sting you?' I asked.

'Yes, thank you,' he said.

'Well, I nearly got stung too,' I replied.

'Is that what all that cackling was about?' Malcolm asked.

'Never you mind,' I retorted.

'They stung me on the knees as well,' he added. 'I suppose when I was crouching down my trousers were tight on my knees and they didn't take long to find my weak spot.'

'So, what do we do with them now?' I asked.

'Put this lot into the back of the van, home, then I'll show you.'

'It'll be from a very safe distance,' I assured him. I climbed into the passenger seat and hoped that any odd bees that might be outside the sacks would stay put until we reached our flat.

We drove to the back entrance of the garden and

parked the van just inside the gates, leaving the headlights on whilst we unloaded the sacks of bees and carried them up to the empty hive. Malcolm then took the sheeting from the van and spread it out in front of the hive, one end resting halfway up the flight board like a white carpet (it should have been a red one with all the effort that had gone into their capture), the rest spread out evenly on the grass. I was intrigued but apprehensive as to what was going to happen next.

Once more Malcolm donned the veil and gloves, but advised me to stand well back – I did not need to be told twice. Then, as requested, I turned off the lights from the van, picked up the torch and directed the beam of light onto the sheet and flight board. Malcolm undid the string on the first sack, which held the most bees, placed the open end just in front of the flight board and gradually eased the heaving mass of bees, comb and honey onto the sheet. He repeated this performance with the other three sacks, spreading their contents behind the first contingent of bees but keeping everything on the sheet. From the light of the torch I could clearly see the bees crawling through, over and round the comb but amazingly making straight for the gentle slope into the beehive. Not one was attempting to fly.

'We'll leave them to it now – you'll be surprised how quickly they'll get themselves organised. I only hope we've managed to catch the queen, otherwise they'll only live for about three days. They must have some contact with the queen at least once a day, without her they are lost. The queen not only rules and gives life to the hive but equally, without the bees she would die, for the queen bee is unable to feed herself and relies completely on her workers to do this for her.'

We went back up to the house, had some supper and were more than happy to sink into our lovely feather bed and let the night take over. The next morning we hurried down to the orchard wondering what we would find. A number of bees were dead in the comb but it was obvious a large number had in fact crawled into the hive.

'I suppose I could have a look inside, but I think I'll leave them in peace for today,' Malcolm pondered. 'Meanwhile, we'd better move all this comb and honey or we'll have robber bees on our hands, and they could attack our bees and I don't think they're strong enough at the moment to take on a pitched battle.'

'What on earth are we going to do with it?' I asked.

'We'll wrap it in polythene for now so that bees, ours or others, can't smell it. I'll bring a churn back from the dairy, then, this evening, we'll put the whole mixture of honey, comb and dead bees into it and pour boiling water over the lot. Hopefully, the wax will melt and float to the top, and once it is set we can skim it off and mix it with paraffin to make the best polish you could possibly have. We'll make mead with the watered down honey that is left – having sieved the dead bees out first, of course.'

There seemed to be no end to my beloved's ideas – crazy or otherwise. We were very fortunate that our landlady did not object to our activities. Not every landlord would be willing to have their house turned into a drink and polish works, but Mrs Eynon was an exceptional person, a very sprightly eighty-eight-year-old, dainty as a wren and as quick in mind if not movement.

Born in London in the late eighteen hundreds, she retained the Londoner's inborn quick wit and humour; although she had lived in Carmarthen for the last fifty years she still yearned for the big city. At the age of nineteen she had married an apprentice cabinet maker who was being taught his craft at Waring and Gillows. The marriage was against the wishes of her parents who considered that she was marrying beneath her station. Her late husband had in fact made the two beautiful Edwardian cabinets that stood in our living room. She still lived and dressed to a bygone era – always in black, calf-length skirts and tiny buttoned ankle boots – goodness knows where she managed to buy them.

In the mornings she wore her long, silver hair pulled back into a tight bun, her blue eyes ever bright in the small, elfin face. In the afternoons, her hair would be swept up on top of her head and secured with black combs; she would change into a high necked dress, usually graced with a marcasite brooch or pearl choker. At four o'clock she would make tea in a silver teapot accompanied with wafer thin bread and butter, Madeira cake or Marie biscuits.

Yes, we were certainly very fortunate to have such a landlady. Mrs Eynon was as eager to see the bees flying in her orchard as we were and was delighted to report to Malcolm that evening, as he leaned on an empty churn that he had just taken from the back of the Bradford van, that the bees had been flying in and out of the hive most of the day.

'If they're still flying in a week's time, we'll know that we have the queen and a good chance of establishing a new colony.' But it was not to be.

The bees did not survive so we were bee-less, but we did earn our five pounds for clearing the roof of livestock and honey, plus the fact that we were able to make about three pounds of polish and five gallons of very drinkable mead.

So really it had been quite a successful exercise, and we had learned a lot about bees. A couple of weeks later I was happily typing when the office manager came in and asked if we were still interested in keeping bees, as there was an elderly man whom he had heard of who was going to get rid of his bees as he had rheumatism and arthritis and could no longer cope with them (so the tale that you do not develop these two complaints if you keep bees was in fact a myth). I immediately said yes of course we were very interested, and asked where the gentleman and his bees lived. Strangely enough, these bees were also in Brechfa. I just hoped he didn't have them in his roof.

Malcolm of course was delighted, and that evening found us once again up in the hills near Brechfa looking for yet another little cottage, but this time with an occupant. We eventually found Mr Lewis, who seemed to be very pleased to have some visitors to whom he could tell his life story. After about three quarters of an hour we managed to steer the conversation round to the subject of bees, whereupon he regaled us with yet more stories.

Eventually he waved his stick in the direction of his vegetable patch, pointing out three rather dilapidated beehives, all of which he assured us were full of gentle but active workers that had been well looked after and only needed to be carefully moved to their new home.

Malcolm asked if any excluders had been placed in position, which had the effect of keeping the bees in the lower sections of the hives. Mr Lewis nodded his balding head vigorously up and down and assured Malcolm *bach* that they had been put into each hive just two weeks ago. A price was agreed, a few further instructions given, then Mr Lewis said that he must go into the house and sit down as his legs were aching. Looking back on that evening however, I think Mr Lewis in fact retreated to the safety of his cottage.

We now had to get down to the business of moving the hives. As it was evening time most of the bees had returned from their wanderings and were all in the bottom two sections of their respective hives and hopefully thinking of going to sleep. Having closed the front of the hives, the idea was to remove the top two sections of each hive, which only contained honey, replace the top, and put the bees that were contained in the lower two sections into the back of the Bradford.

I put on one of the veils and watched from a safe distance whilst Malcolm, complete with veil and gloves, removed the rotting top of the first hive. Unfortunately, the veil caught on the corner of the roof of the hive, which pulled the veil to one side. Had the excluder been in position as we had been told it was, all would have been well. But there wasn't an excluder (fib number one). The hive was certainly full of very active bees, to the brim in fact, but gentle? No (fib number two). The bees thrust themselves angrily straight up into Malcolm's veil. He very quickly pulled it straight and replaced the top of the hive but not before some sixty to eighty bees had been trapped inside the black veiling and goodness knows how many others were trying to get in at the enemy who had dared to disturb their home.

I watched frightened and horrified as Malcolm stumbled towards me, followed by an enormous black cloud of angry Welsh bees. I quickly jumped into the van, opened the door ready for Malcolm to get in as quickly as possible, and slammed it hard to keep out as many bees as we could.

'We must get to a doctor quickly,' he panted (as if I needed telling); the effect of so many bee stings in the head was already affecting his breathing, balance and vision.

Unfortunately, at that time I could not drive, so Malcolm started the van and we headed downhill towards the village of Nantgaredig and hopefully a doctor.

Malcolm was fast losing consciousness and I just prayed we would reach the village safely before he passed out completely. We must have been some three hundred yards from the bottom of the hill when I saw another car coming towards us. What was I to do? If I grabbed the wheel to steer to the left, we stood a good chance of going over a steep drop – Malcolm's natural reaction to my interference with the steering would be to steer to the right and we would be pretty certain of hitting the other car. We were practically on a head-on collision course with Malcolm almost unconscious and completely unaware (even to this day) that another vehicle was anywhere near us. As luck would have it a small bumpy verge appeared at the crucial moment and the other car passed us, bumping over the uneven turf and stones with much verbal abuse and fist shaking. We did not stop. Some sixty seconds later I shouted at Malcolm to stop. We had reached the village and the first house. Malcolm stopped all right but then passed out completely.

Our guardian angel was on duty that night – a well-rubbed brass plate on the gate declared 'Dr J Lyle, GP'. I ran round to Malcolm's door pulled it open and tried to drag him out of the car, but he was far too heavy. So, I tore up the garden path and banged and banged on the big brass knocker.

Our arrival had not gone unnoticed, for the door was

opened almost immediately by I assumed Doctor Lyle himself. 'Quick, quick, please hurry, it's my husband,' I implored, tugging at his arm.

'Young lady,' he said, gently but firmly removing my hand from his sleeve, I do not treat drunks.' I suppose we did look a strange pair. I still had my bee veil on, as did my poor unconscious Malcolm.

'He isn't drunk,' I almost screamed, 'he's been stung by hundreds of bees.'

'Well now, that's a different thing altogether; we'll get him into the surgery then we can sort him out.'

Between us we half dragged, half carried Malcolm into the doctor's surgery and propped him against the wall.

'A shot of adrenalin is the answer,' said Doctor Lyle, plus something I didn't quite catch the name of. It certainly did the trick; in less than a minute Malcolm was completely back to normal.

'I should think a glass of whisky would be in order now young man, and if I were you, I should go home and forget about bee-keeping,' said the doctor as he removed some sixty-nine bee sting sacs from Malcolm's neck, eyelids, ears, scalp and face.

He then poured a triple whisky for himself and Malcolm. I apparently only qualified for a single whisky as I only had ten stings, not that I was complaining. I was in complete agreement about forgetting all about bee-keeping; it would be much easier and healthier to buy honey from a shop or some other bee-keeper. But that was all wishful thinking – I should have known better.

We thanked Doctor Lyle for his help and then... headed back to the bees.

Two of the hives did in fact have excluders in place and were loaded into the back of the Bradford van with little more than a few puffs and grunts. The bees that had given us so much trouble were driven into the depths of the hive with generous clouds of smoke, and because it was almost dark they were much quieter. The excluder was put in place and that hive was taken to the orchard three days later.

We felt that we were real bee-keepers now that we owned three hives full of very hard working bees – but gentle? Never. They were the most bad-tempered bees that we ever kept in our twenty odd years of beekeeping.

Taking the honey from these particular bees was always exciting, to say the least. The first year we didn't extract the honey from the comb but let the bees keep it for their winter feed, plus some extra thick syrup to keep them happy, or should I say, happier.

The second year that we had bees, they were placed at the far end of the vegetable patch at Fronlas and come August the three 'supers', or top sections from each hive were removed and wrapped in polythene to contain the smell of the honey, prevent leakage, and also to stop the bees from robbing us of their honey.

We only had the 'honey parcels' in the shed for one night before we took them down to the dairy to extract the honey, but the bees buzzed the shed constantly and stung anything that moved within fifty yards of their hive for five days. We were practically confined to barracks. Consequently, if I wanted any vegetables from the garden I could have done with a suit of armour for protection. As it was I would first put on a bobble hat, then my maternity coat, the mandarin collar being buttoned on top of my head instead of round my neck; rubber gloves to protect my hands as I pushed them through the pockets to pick runner beans which I could see through the button holes – plus of course two pairs of trousers and high waders. I could hardly move, but I did not get stung. Potatoes were more of a problem as it was more difficult to see the ground through the button holes; I'm sure the bees knew this as I always managed to get stung whilst digging potatoes – one of my handicaps being my rubber gloves, which always seemed to flop down over my hands, revealing my wrists, for there were always at least three bees ready to take advantage.

I remember a few years later when we were living in Buckinghamshire, the bees decided to swarm at about eleven o'clock on a lovely sunny morning. They settled in an apple tree in the garden. I immediately telephoned Malcolm who was at the factory in Aylesbury, some fourteen miles away. Unfortunately, he had meetings practically all day and would not be able to do anything with the bees until about four in the afternoon. Normally the old queen leaves the hive, taking half of the inmates with her, all loaded with enough honey to last them three days, so usually they are fairly docile with all the extra weight on board. The queen often settles within thirty yards of the hive for about an hour, whilst the bees that she is taking with her cluster tightly round her in the shape of a rugby ball, before flying off in search of a new abode.

Sometimes we've been lucky and the bees have taken over an empty hive in the garden, that we always have ready for newcomers. But, it was always Malcolm's job to actually deal with the bees.

I was quite happy to turn the extractor handle; to wash jars; to make polish; to make mead; to cut the comb to let the honey run; to make up syrup for the bees' winter food. But I can honestly say I do not care very much for the actual creature.

However, I digress a little. On this sunny afternoon, Malcolm busy with meetings at the factory thus unable to attend to the bees, it was my lot to try and keep the bees on our premises.

So, I banged saucepan lids together, blew the dog whistle and sprayed water from the hosepipe all around them hoping that the noise and the thought of 'bad weather' would send them back to their hold hive or better still into the empty hive. But no such luck.

The bees stayed in the apple tree until half past three, then took off like a whirlwind; presumably the queen leading, the rest following in a huge funnel shaped cloud. I took chase dressed in shorts, tee shirt and flip flops.

Through the hedge in our garden, across a newly-ploughed field, through another hedge, over a stile, through a small wood, across yet another field (full of cows and cow pats). Needless to say, by this time the bees were well out in front. Then I came upon a deep, water-filled ditch; by the time I had negotiated that obstacle, and a thick hedge, and made it to the road, there was not a bee to be seen, only… two workmen who were cleaning the roadside ditch.

You can imagine their surprise and possible alarm at my appearance from the hedge, covered in mud, cow dung and scratches, puffing like a steam engine and enquiring if they'd seen a swarm of bees pass this way. Neither of them spoke, but both nodded their heads vigorously from side to side.

I could see the funny side of the whole situation and started laughing, which did not help. I knew that if I didn't go back through the hedge pretty quickly, I'd probably have hysterics on the spot. A local mental home was only two miles up the road and I think the two workmen clearly thought that I had truly 'lost my bearings'.

There was no point in going on, so I returned home, sorry to have lost a good swarm of bees, but I had tried. So many bees and so many incidents, like Malcolm 'allowing' me to drive the van with two dogs and two hives of live, loud humming bees all the way from Carmarthen to Buckinghamshire because he could handle our new car better than I could and if I bumped the old van it wouldn't matter so much. It was like sitting on a bomb all the way to Aylesbury, hoping that no idiot would bump into me and set loose one hundred thousand bees, two dogs and a raving idiot. Like carrying those same bees from the van to their resting place in a field late that same pitch black night (with me holding the front of the hive) and when I ventured the thought that I was sure that there were bees crawling on my hands, was promptly told that I was over imaginative and it was probably long grass brushing against me as we manoeuvred our way gently across the field. 'Besides,' said my husband, from the back of the hive, 'the front is closed tight.' It wasn't. After we had gently lowered the hive onto the ground, I found dozens of bees crawling all over my hands and arms.

Malcolm said he realised that the bees were escaping but he knew that if he said anything, I would have probably dropped the lot. As it was, I nearly went into orbit anyway.

Like when a very strong swarm of wild bees left their huge, hollow oak tree that stood about half a mile away, flew across the valley into our garden, killed off our weakest colony of bees, took over their hive, swept all the dead bodies out onto the flight board and left the old queen to one side with a sting in her thorax. A very dramatic entry, but those bees were the hardest workers of all, producing over one hundredweight of honey each season.

Like the time Malcolm had his leg in plaster and insisted on doing some weeding on all fours in the vegetable garden. He eventually came into the house when it was nearly dark and said, 'Go down to the beehives (we had five at the time), listen to each one then come back and tell me what you can hear.' So, still the ever obedient wife, off I stumbled in the dusk to the back of the hives, bending low to tune in to each one. Number one hive gave off the normal hum of activity as bees worked in the hive and beat their wings to cool the air inside the hive. The same low drone came from hives two and three; but at number four hive, although there was the normal resonant throbbing, there was also a high pitched piping, which would stop for a few seconds and then be followed by a low pitched piping.

This happened several times. What on earth was happening inside number four? I galloped back up to the house, delighted that I had obviously heard whatever it was that was certainly unusual. As Malcolm was not very mobile he suggested that I take the small tape recorder and record the bleeps in the hope that we would be able to find out exactly what they meant.

The next day the bees in the piping hive split and swarmed. It was many months and reference books later that we had confirmed that the piping was in fact the two queens calling the bees to take sides before the departure of the old queen.

A fascinating hobby with those woolly, six legged insects quite rightly named bees. No other word could describe them better.

Chapter Seven

I was settling well into the pig farming life. The birth of
the little ones always a wonder and delight (well, nearly
always). The tenderness and agility of the most awkward
of sows always amazed me. We preferred to let the sows
furrow out in the field whenever possible as they seemed
happier without the restrictions of the indoor pens. Most
of our sows in the early stages of our pig-keeping days
were either basic Large Whites or Welsh cross – good
strong, healthy, prolific and practically trouble free
(healthwise that is) pigs. But then there was our Landrace, a new model. In theory it should have been the pig
breeders' dream; extra long in the back: not so prone to
carrying excess fat as in the case of the Large White –
hence better meat grading; average litters of eight; and
ears that covered their eyes, thus making them much
easier to catch than the far-seeing, crafty Large White. We
found the extra length in the back of the Landrace was
their weak spot, which put extra strain on their back legs
and for some reason seemed to make them prone to
rheumatism – they really could have done with an extra
pair of legs in the middle. True, they did not make excess
fat, but took considerably longer to make the correct
weight.

On top of that they were not happy pigs – nervous
and neurotic, not very good mothers and they certainly
did not have the characters of the normal, ordinary farm
pig.

Our prize Landrace was due to produce and was out with the other sows roaming our four fields. We were well into October and had returned from a dinner party just after midnight. It was a lovely moonlight night with a fairly brisk wind blowing which drove fluffy, silver clouds scurrying across the dark sky.

'We'd better go and check the Landrace,' said Malcolm as he opened the front door, 'just in case she's started, though she looked all right at teatime but you can never tell. I'll take Mrs Jones home first (our ever faithful babysitter, who lived next to the church just three fields away) whilst you put the kettle on for a cup of tea.'

Malcolm was only gone for five minutes and we decided to have the tea after we had checked the sow. We put on Wellington boots, started across the field in front of the house and stumbled over to the old oak and the tall ash trees under which the sows usually slept in a great snoring, heaving, heap. We counted eight snouts and tails but no Landrace sow was amongst them. So down we went to the lower field, looking well under the hedges all the way to the stream. Sows often furrow near a hedge for protection and because a bank will conveniently form part of the rough nest that most sows try to make. Still no sign of her. We then started searching along the banks of the stream just in case the silly animal had got herself into difficulties near the water. Sure enough, she'd made a nest right on the bank and had in fact already produced one skinny little piglet, which she was pummelling with her long nose.

'Hm,' said Malcolm thoughtfully, 'well, she can't stay there, they'll all end up in the water.' Should we drive her back up to the sties or what? She had to be moved away from the stream, wherever her final farrowing place was to be, and the only way to get her mobile was to carry her first offspring about twelve inches from her nose and encourage her to follow it and us back up the field. We managed to coax her about fifty yards from the stream when she decided to give birth to another skinny piglet. It arrived exactly as it should. Toes and nose first, very pink and slippery. We guided the two new arrivals onto the ample milk supply, rubbed the sow's very large tummy and told her we would like another eight please.

'I think we had better watch her, so will you take the first or second watch?' Malcolm asked.

'I think I would prefer the first watch,' I ventured – I like to go to bed and stay there. The thought of getting out of a lovely warm bed after a doze of only two hours did not really appeal to the dormouse in me.

So, back to the house and a quick change into my old working clothes, enough time to pick up a torch, a *Reader's Digest* (in case I had time to read in between piglets – one never knew how long they would take to arrive), and a bucket to sit on. Malcolm went to bed and I retraced my steps to the bottom field to watch our pedigree sow. Still only two piglets – the time one thirty.

Sitting on an upturned bucket waiting for the next piglet to arrive, I had time to listen to the swish of an owl's wings as it dipped and glided between the trees. A fox calling a vixen – the eerie 'Yark, yark' – was instant encouragement to flash my torch along the banks of the stream, through the branches of the high oaks and elms then back in a circle to the empty field behind me… Just in case. (I don't know what at, but just in case.)

Then, the next piglet arrived – backwards; the head was covered with a caul, which I promptly removed. The sow meanwhile was doing its best to trample the first two piglets to death. I deftly lifted the little creatures out of harm's way and held the three of them until the mother settled down, then put them down at the milk bar where they happily sucked away until the arrival of number four. This time head first, again with a caul and again the mother did her best imitation of Nellie the elephant gone berserk.

After two hours, eight piglets had been born, tail first without a caul, head first with a caul, none in the ortho-dox manner and all accompanied by a frantic *pas de deux* by the mother.

I decided that it was time for the second watch to come on parade. I hurried back to the house, made a pot of tea and dutifully presented a cup to my sleeping spouse.

'Come on, darling, wake up. It's your turn to watch the sow,' I said brightly – shaking darling's shoulder. 'I've made you a cup of tea before you go out.'

'How many has she had?' he grunted – sounding not unlike the creature I had just left in the field.

'Eight,' I replied – feeling quite pleased with myself.

'Well, if she's had eight, she can manage the rest her-self,' he mumbled, and turned over and went back to sleep. And she did. We had a good even litter of ten with no help from Malcolm – just the sow and I.

Little piglets look much more attractive after about four or five days, as is the case with most newly-born creatures (the exception being the human baby, which I do not really find at all appealing until they are about three months old at the earliest). By then, the mother has settled into a relaxed routine; the little piglets know exactly where the food is and which teat is theirs, which is amazing when there may be as many as fourteen in a litter; in fact, that was the highest number in a litter that we actually raised. We had one sow that gave birth to twenty-three, but there were many casualties. A good even litter of ten is the most satisfactory number, though I believe at the moment the national average is eight.

We used to castrate the male piglets when they were between ten and twenty days old, but nowadays they are left to grow to maturity, complete. On the appointed day my vegetable knife was duly sharpened (why Malcolm could not have his own knife for the job I do not know; I normally cut my finger on my newly-sharpened blade for the next two weeks or until I had managed to blunt it enough on carrots, swedes and onions on my chopping board). There were two large bowls of well salted water at the ready (Malcolm's cure for all cuts, colds, bites and pig operations), one bowl for cleansing the area around the necessary parts to be removed and one bowl for swabbing after the deed had been done, plus some clean sheeting and cotton wool. We were ready. As soon as Malcolm picked up a piglet from the pen by its back legs, it would squeal non-stop until I held it firmly upside down with its head and body jammed between my legs and we were ready to do the deed. Not a squirm or a squeak as it was cleansed, cut, swabbed and returned to the pen, back with its mother, brothers and sisters. We never had any infection problems and they would all run about the pen as if nothing had happened.

When the piglets are between six and eight weeks old, they are weaned from their mother (who is taken to the boar for service), then they are left in peace to grow into lean pork chops and succulent joints. I have often been asked if I became upset when it was time for the pigs to go to the abattoir. The answer is no. With so many being reared in fairly large groups, plus the fact that you only have contact with them for a maximum of four months, they do not have the time to establish themselves as individual characters. It is quite a different story with the sows who could be with you for as much as ten years.

One sow, a Welsh Black, was an excellent mother, but whenever she was weaned from her litter and put out into the field, she would try to get back into the sty with her young ones, and on three occasions managed to release over fifty pigs in her endeavours to reach her own litter. She did this by lifting the pigsty gates off their hinges on five pens. The chaos caused by fifty pigs of various sizes on the rampage over one's vegetable patch is enough to put one off gardening for life. Not to mention the fact that one has practically to be a fully trained athlete, of the cross country variety, to cope with galloping across fields, through hedges and over ditches in order to round up fifty pigheaded pigs.

Another sow, a Large White crossed with a Welsh Black and consequently covered with many black spots which made her look like a king-sized Dalmatian, would spend all day rattling a stone around in her mouth, dropping it at feeding time only to pick it up again immediately after she had finished her food.

Then there was Hoppy, who always walked on three legs – despite many examinations, professional and otherwise, nothing was ever found to be wrong with her fourth leg. Loppy Lugs, the Welsh cross, had the longest ears you could imagine, completely covering her eyes so that she could only see the ground immediately under her nose unless she strained her head right back and peered down that long hairy snout. It was this particular sow that on one occasion caused me more than a little anxiety.

It was a Saturday morning and I wanted to pop into Carmarthen to do some extra shopping for a dinner party we were giving that evening. I had allowed Malcolm to persuade me to take Loppy Lugs to Pibwrlloyd for a service.

'It's only a small detour,' he coaxed, 'you only have to drive two miles the other side of Carmarthen and leave the sow with the boar. It won't take more than ten minutes at the most and you could leave the trailer there so that you don't have to worry about parking it in town.'

It was not much to ask, besides he would be looking after the children and to go shopping without them was always a treat.

We loaded Loppy Lugs into the trailer, which Malcolm had made especially for the job of transporting the sows. It was about six feet long, four feet wide and three feet or so high; a comfortable fit for a sow with not quite enough space for her to turn round, which meant she would be loaded nose first but would have to back out to get out (so the theory went). Once inside, a metal top was wedged into the sides and then firmly roped down. The back of the trailer could be lowered without undoing all the rope, as this was held in position with two bolts. Malcolm walked around the trailer for a final inspection, tapped the side and said, 'You'll be fine, and don't forget to ask which day we should pick up the Large White sow, she should have been served by now.'

I waved goodbye to Malcolm and the children and drove off as steadily as I could, pulling the bumping trailer and its large occupant, who no doubt was doing her best to keep her balance. I stopped briefly to pick up an elderly lady at Peniel who was waiting for the Carmarthen bus. This lady (we never found out her name) would cycle on an old-fashioned sit-up-and-beg bicycle from Peniel to a farm situated about a mile further up the hill from Fronlas. Going to the farm was a slow journey for her as it was uphill practically all the way but, on her return trip she would just sit on the large saddle and go like the wind, which meant that she would pass our gate at about thirty miles an hour or more. We were forever concerned that one of the sows would break through the hedge and cross the narrow road just at the wrong moment. I do not know who would have come off worse, the sow being hit at such a speed or the elderly cyclist thumping into a four-hundred-pound pork joint.

Little did my passenger know as she sat chatting beside me that basically, she was the reason for the payment of an annual insurance premium, paid to protect her, us and the pigs.

We arrived at the Llandilo turning on the outskirts of Carmarthen to find ourselves in a small traffic jam. The road was being dug up yet again, with the person in charge of traffic control not knowing whether he should be waving cars through or stopping them. I was convinced the council gave applicants for the post an IQ test, and the one with the lowest was given the job.

We were at the junction for about fifteen minutes, during which time I knew the sow behind me was getting restless as I could feel the trailer bar juddering on the car hitch.

I thought that I had better have a little peep to see exactly what Loppy Lugs was doing. I peered through the slatted sides and could see that she had her nose pushed hard against the top of the trailer where about an inch of daylight was seeping into the darkened container. I poked her hard on the nose through the little space and eased the top over to cover the small gap. If only I could keep the car moving we would be all right.

Unfortunately, it was not possible. Some cars were waved through but we were only actually able to move about twenty yards before being forced to stop again. I looked in the mirror and could see the tip of the sow's snout testing the air between the metal top and the front of the trailer. Even as I leapt out of the car, she pushed her nose through the gap and lifted the top of the trailer clear of the sides with the top of her head. The rope that was supposed to be holding the roof of the trailer in position was festooned around the sides, absolutely useless. I did not have time to wonder why or what had happened, I was more concerned with how to keep the lid on the sow.

I called to my elderly passenger to give me a hand, which she willingly did. I hoped the effort involved would not give her a heart attack. The problem was that we needed more hands. The old lady was hanging on to her side of the trailer and I was hanging on to my side but we were little match for a very large sow that had decided it would rather be out than in. The 'lid' was getting higher and higher. The cars in the hold up were now being waved through; if we could just hold on, perhaps when the traffic came to a standstill again, someone would be able to give us a hand.

The first help came from a motorcyclist who could clearly see our predicament as he was stopped by the red flag and came to a halt at our side. He quickly summoned a couple of men from the waiting cars who were able to hold the tin roof down, thus keeping the sow contained, but all decided that the rope was not really strong enough to do the job (in fact it had rubbed through on the side of the trailer). I think it probably was strong enough but I was so frightened by now that the sow might get out onto the road and into the traffic that I was sure the only way would be to chain her down.

It is incredible, but as if in answer to my thoughts and prayers a scrap iron merchant whom we had met on a couple of occasions appeared in the stream of traffic driving his lorry which was loaded with… scrap iron. Quickly sizing up the situation, he produced from the rusting jumble of metal a length of chain which was just long enough to go round the trailer once with much pulling, tugging and knot tying.

I was assured by all the helpers that they thought that I should now be able to finish the journey without further mishap. To my embarrassment but relief, all the traffic was held up so that I could make a clean getaway and keep going. I suppose even the dozy traffic controller did not want a sow cavorting around to add to his problems. Everyone cheered as I pulled away with my four-legged cargo hopefully well and truly secured.

I made a very brief stop to let my elderly passenger escape into town with the parting words that she would be having tea with a friend and would not need a lift home. I did not know if this was true or not, but I could not blame her if in fact it was a small fib. I then drove swiftly over the Towey bridge and headed straight for Pibwrlloyd Farm. It was a great comfort to see that Olwyn was on duty that day. He was always very helpful and I knew that Loppy Lugs would be unloaded and put into the right pen with little trouble. She was. I could not help noticing however, as the bolt on the gate was pushed into position that there were more sows in the pens than normal, and said so to Olwyn.

'Yes, we're up to capacity at the moment,' he said. 'In fact, I'm quite pleased to see you; perhaps you could take your Large White sow back with you? We would then have an extra pen.'

My heart sank and my stomach seemed to turn inside out. 'Are you sure she's been served?' I asked – hoping he might have some doubt, in which case he would have to keep her for a positive service.

'Oh yes – she's been served three times.' I could see there was no way out – I would have to take the sow home. So I arranged to leave the trailer at the farm whilst I did my shopping and promised to be back in about an hour. So much for my morning of carefree shopping. I galloped round the shops at breakneck speed, picking up last minute bits and pieces for the evening's dinner party, arriving back at Pibwrlloyd at half past twelve.

I hitched on the trailer and backed it in line with the pen that contained our Large White sow, Donk – so named because she was the size of a small donkey with the strength of a mule in her huge shoulders. Her ears looked not unlike two receivers from Jodrell Bank and were just as acute.

She plodded slowly and deliberately up the sloping back of the trailer which I had let down for the purpose. Once she was inside, I quickly lifted up the back and slammed it tight behind her, dropping the holding bolts firmly into position. Olwyn pushed the top down firmly, then took the rope over and under the trailer from front to back twice, and the chain completely around the trailer. I fervently hoped that I would reach home without too much trouble; in fact, no trouble at all if possible.

I drove through Carmarthen without a hitch, but as I

was driving up the hill towards Peniel I could again see through the reversing mirror a snout easing its way between the top and sides of the trailer. Even as I watched mesmerised, the sow's head, feet and shoulders appeared, and within seconds she was hanging over the front of the trailer. I jammed on my brakes, which threw her off balance, making her fall back into the trailer; unfortunately, she took the top section of one of the sides in with her.

I raced round to the trailer to see how best to contain her, but it was hopeless; the rope had rubbed through again and the rusty chain had broken in half. The top of the trailer had somehow managed to fall inside the trailer and was standing end-on, resting against the unbroken side. She could quite easily have stepped over the damaged side, but was still facing the front and was apparently in a bit of a daze. I knew that I would not be able to rope everything together, so I jumped back into the car and made a hard racing start which made the sow slide to the back of the trailer. I then drove at sixty miles an hour, swerving across the road whenever possible so that she would have to concentrate on her balance.

For five miles I drove in the worst possible manner, before pulling into the sanctuary of our yard. I was still shaking with fright as I told Malcolm what had happened and said that if he wanted the sows taken to the boar or collected in the future, he could do it himself; the trailer was his construction and he would have made it more secure. He eventually calmed me down with soft talk and a cup of tea, but not before Donk had scrambled over the side of the trailer and helped herself to a large quantity of cabbage from Malcolm's vegetable patch. Perhaps there was a little bit of justice there.

I had recovered by the evening and was able to laugh about the whole escapade with our guests. The design of the trailer was modified and never again did we have any problems with the transporting of our sows.

Chapter Eight

That autumn, we decided that we would succumb to buying a television set. We were warned that in all probability the picture would not be very clear as the signal would be screened by the hills around us. Malcolm, however, did not seem to think this would be too much of a problem.

'We can always put an aerial up in the top field,' he said nonchalantly, as if it would be no more trouble than making a cup of tea.

'I would have thought it would have to be quite a large construction,' I ventured. 'If you have to erect a very high pole to put the aerial on, you are bound to need fairly hefty guy ropes to hold the thing in position.'

Malcolm would not be drawn. 'We'll wait until the set arrives, see how good or bad the picture is and then make a decision.'

The set arrived on a Saturday morning. An ordinary aerial was clamped to the chimney stack on the end of the house by the television engineer as part and parcel of the purchase. 'I don't rate your chances of receiving a very good picture,' he muttered as he prepared to switch on our latest acquisition. No glorious colour set for us – just black, white and grey. The screen showed us white blobs on a black background, white lines on a grey background; in fact, a fairly comprehensive selection of various boring patterns, all accompanied by a crackly, swishing sound.

'Is that it?' I asked the engineer.

'I would hope to be able to improve on that,' he answered with a smile.

'It's a case of swinging the aerial around to see which direction the signal is strongest.'

I sincerely hoped he could improve on what could be seen at the moment, otherwise we would never know whether we were watching the news or Andy Pandy, unless of course we consulted the *Radio and TV Times*.

I soon became bored with watching the black and white moving patterns so left Malcolm and the engineer to find a picture by themselves. After about an hour, I ventured into the sitting room to enquire if they would like a cup of coffee, and what was the picture situation.

'Yes, we'd love a cup of coffee, and the picture is about as good as we can get at the moment.' said Malcolm.

'A set sometimes takes a couple of days to settle down,' the engineer explained somewhat apologetically. 'It could well improve on what you see now, plus the fact that a picture can vary in different weather conditions. For example, it could be clearer in dry weather than in wet.'

A fat lot of good that was, I thought, knowing how much it rained in West Wales; I practically had webbed feet myself. I looked hard at the picture on the screen – it was a preview of one of the afternoon's sporting events. Was it really snowing that hard at the Kempton Park race course? After all it was still early autumn. There are times when it is best not to voice a true opinion and… this was such a time.

'Well, it is a wet day and as you say, it may well produce a clearer picture in a few days' time,' I said, hoping that I did not sound too pessimistic; after all, it was not the engineer's fault that we lived in the back of beyond, surrounded by hills.

It rained the whole of the following week and needless to say, the picture did not improve. Seven days though gave Malcolm time to think up ways of boosting our aerial.

Saturday dawned, the rain had stopped and the weekend was declared a 'let's get the television aerial sorted out' weekend. The idea of putting an aerial in the top field was abandoned. It would (as I previously suggested) have to be quite a construction; there was the problem of the wire cable, which would have to be supported for about one hundred and thirty yards and be out of the reach of the cows and pigs, plus the fact that the longer the cable, the weaker the signal.

'I wondered if we could fix the aerial to the top of the oak tree by the barn,' said Malcolm. 'That would give us a boost of about twenty feet on what we have at the moment.'

We studied the large oak tree carefully. The trunk was straight enough for about fifteen feet before branching in three directions. It was going to be pretty well nigh impossible to secure the aerial with anything like enough stability to the waving branches which spread outwards rather than up.

Malcolm was not one to give up easily. 'I still think the oak tree's the answer,' he said quietly. We looked at the oak from every angle. 'How about if we put a scaffolding pole at the top?' Malcolm said half to himself, 'then we could…' He did not finish the sentence.

'That's it. That's it,' he said excitedly. 'I could drill out a three inch hole into the top of the trunk the width of the pole, drive in four six inch nails into the hole, wedge the pole in the hole over the nails, which would give extra stability, then peg out guy ropes from the top of the pole just below where the aerial would be strapped. It would be about thirty feet higher than it is now; the cable could easily go under the eaves into the roof and down into the lounge.'

Hopefully our problem was now solved – it was action time. The rest of the morning and afternoon was taken up with removing the aerial from its former resting place on the side of the chimney and installing it into the top of the tree. The most awkward and delicate job was hauling the scaffolding pole – complete with aerial strapped to its side, guy ropes dangling – up through the branches of the oak tree. With much manoeuvring and puffing, and many muttered expletives, we eventually managed to ease the pole into position and secure the guy ropes. We stood back and surveyed our handiwork.

The large aitch-shaped aerial rose firmly above the oak. So far, so good. The question was, did we now have a better picture after all the effort that had gone into putting up the aerial? We would soon see. We made a cup of tea and took it into the lounge for the big 'switch on'. The quiet click did not seem much to mark the climax to such an operation, but perhaps it was just as well for there was no improvement whatsoever to the jumble of black, white and grey patterns. Poor Malcolm looked so downcast.

'I just can't understand it,' he sighed, but still with that puzzled look that meant that he had not given up yet. We drank our tea in relative silence, the only sound being the shushing from the television set. Suddenly, Malcolm jumped up and raced out of the door. I followed as quickly as I could and just caught the words '…wrong direction.' He disappeared round the corner of the house and headed for the old oak tree. He released the slippery guy ropes of the aerial then shinned the fifteen feet up the tree to where the scaffolding pole rested in the drilled out hole.

'Right,' he called from his lofty perch, 'open the lounge window so that you can see the television set from outside and shout out to me when the picture improves, we obviously haven't set the aerial in the right direction.'

With much gentle tugging, twisting and turning, Malcolm gradually eased the twenty-foot scaffolding pole, complete with aerial, through three hundred and sixty degrees, with me shouting out every few seconds, 'better, better, better' or 'worse, worse, gone'. The picture appeared and disappeared with varying degrees of clarity. We eventually settled on a line running north east to south west, not giving a perfect picture, but at least one that was watchable. The guy ropes were fastened in their new positions and again we returned to the lounge to view our handiwork. Yes, we would certainly be able to watch Paul Temple that evening and be quite certain of being able to identify 'who did it'. We were very pleased with our bit of civil engineering.

The set behaved itself quite well for several weeks, then one November evening we were stretched out by the fire watching our favourite television serial, Maigret, whilst a gale howled, pushed and clawed at every angle to our little house. The rain poured down the windows in sheets as if straight from a fireman's hosepipe, and the television set reverted to its old habit of rolling indistinct patterns of grey up and down the screen.

'I bet this heavy wind has blown the aerial off the main signal direction,' exclaimed Malcolm.

'Oh well, we can sort it out tomorrow,' I replied (will I never learn?).

'Come on. Let's just give it a try. Put a coat over your head and stand by the window as you did before, and I'll zap up the tree and pull the aerial round.'

'What, in these conditions?' I wailed.

'Yes,' said Malcolm giving me a push in the direction of the door. So, out in the pouring rain, I stood with a coat over my head, trying desperately to see if the picture on the television set improved, whilst the wind hurled the curtains round the open window in all directions and my crazy, pig-headed husband shinned up a slippery tree to twist a twenty foot scaffolding pole in all directions of the compass. He could so easily fall and break his neck and I could catch pneumonia – all this just so that we could see the end of Maigret.

Malcolm did not fall out of the tree. The picture was restored but we did not see the end of Maigret. I would have to wait a couple of days to see if I developed pneumonia. 'Was it ever worth it?' I asked my beloved as I put my cold feet on him that night in bed.

'Yes, of course it was,' he grunted. 'If it happens again we can put it right even in the worst of conditions, and take your cold feet off my legs, talking doesn't dull my senses, you know.'

'I should have left you up the tree,' I moaned. 'After all, I wouldn't have got cold feet if I hadn't been standing outside for such a long time in polar conditions.'

'It wasn't exactly snowing.'

'Well, it jolly well felt like an arctic blizzard.' I eventually fell asleep, hoping that we would not have too many hurricanes whilst watching television.

Chapter Nine

The elements played a major role in our life at Fronlas, but I suppose that must be the case for all folk who live in the country and depend on nature to produce the right conditions for whatever job is in hand. Just normal routine can be affected by just basic Welsh drizzle, a phenomenon which could last for weeks, making the quarry tiles on the ground floor absolutely lethal to walk on, the wallpaper to hang away from the walls, and all clothes, even though stored in wardrobes and cupboards, would sop up the moist atmosphere like dried out sponges. On the other hand, a really good downpour would send the water roaring down the top field, through the hay barn (the bottom bales were never any good, not even for bedding) into the pigsties, fortunately flooding through the gullies and not where the pigs slept in tidy piles, before cascading down the road, taking the corner of the dung heap with it for good measure. Sometimes we would not have rain for weeks, in which case the well would practically run dry and we would find ourselves hauling water in ten gallon churns from the factory.

I remember one spring Malcolm decided that we would plough and reseed the bottom fields so that with luck we would make enough hay to see our five assorted head of cattle through their winter needs. Willi, our good neighbour who lived at Hafod, the adjoining farm, seemed as enthusiastic as we were to see the fields of

Fronlas improved, and was quite happy to let us have any machinery we needed at any time as long as he was not wanting it for himself; this arrangement worked very well, as most of our farming had to be done before eight in the morning, after five thirty in the evening, on Saturday or Sunday, and when the weather was right. On looking back, we were expecting a great deal from our unpredictable climate.

Malcolm borrowed Willi's little grey Ferguson twenty-seven tractor and a two-furrow plough to open up and turn the soil. Three early mornings and three late evenings completed that job. Discing the field in all directions to make a fine tilth on which the seed could be sown took another three sessions – the lower half of the field taking more time to break down as it was inclined to be rather wet, consequently the earth was inclined to coagulate in large unyielding lumps. Eventually Malcolm said he could not work the soil any longer; if the seed was not sown quickly it would be too late and we would not be able to take a hay crop this summer.

We then borrowed a fiddle from Willi to enable us to sow the seed evenly. It looked a bit like a wooden bucket with a calico top, which held the seed, with different sized holes in the base set on a moving disc above a wooden bow. Moving one's arm like a violin player would spin the seed to the left and right for approximately six feet in each direction. Malcolm set the first markers at twelve feet intervals across the top and bottom of the field before making a straight line to each one, sowing the seed as he went.

My job was to gallop across the field with a bucket of seed to refill his empty fiddle whenever he shouted, or to move the markers to their new position wherever he pointed – all this so that there would not be any gaps in our new lay.

The sowing operation was followed by three hours of rolling, pushing the new seed well into the soil. So far so good. We felt very pleased with our efforts and certainly the newly-cultivated earth gave a 'cared for' look to the field which it did not have before, when it only sported nettles and thistles and of course marsh grass in the lower part of the field.

We inspected our bit of farming daily, looking anxiously for the first tiny blades of green, to show that we had a good take. It was seventeen days before we could definitely say that we could see sown grass growing and not new weeds. The leaves were so fine that the soil looked as if it had been colour washed with a delicate fall of crème de menthe. But growing it was, and miraculously weather conditions were ideal, and the grass responded well.

When it had reached the height of six inches, Malcolm said that we should now give the field a good dressing of fertiliser in the shape of nitro-chalk pellets. Rather than ask Willi if we could borrow his equipment yet again, it was decided that this was a job that I could do whilst Malcolm was at the dairy. I would use the same method as seed fiddling, but using a bucket, and my hands; setting out markers with twelve feet between each and when I had emptied the bucket set another marker so that when I started again (after refilling my bucket with fertiliser), I would not over or under fertilise any parts of the field. In fact, do the lot myself. I was soon to learn that most of Malcolm's jobs covering this operation, would be on wheels with a seat, whilst I was definitely the infantry, land-based and on foot. Even so it was most satisfying to be able to carry out a complete job, even if I did have to do my own fetching and carrying.

When the grass had reached the height of twelve inches, we had our first hiccup. We had had several really warm days but now it was tending to become rather humid.

'We really do need some rain to clear the air,' Malcolm remarked as we went to bed that night.

At three o'clock in the morning we were suddenly awakened by a tremendous loud bang; it was as if a bomb had exploded directly above the house. We both sat bolt upright in bed like a couple of jack-in-the-boxes. The room was filled with a bright blue light, illuminating everything, crystal clear; in seconds the light was gone, leaving us with the nose-tingling smell of ozone. Malcolm raced to the window, I was but a split second behind him – we both thought the house must be on fire. We looked into the darkness of the field. Nothing. We ran downstairs, into each room. Nothing. Everything was normal except for the strange lingering smell. We were obviously not in any danger and decided that a thunderbolt must have struck the field; there was nothing to be done, so we went back to sleep.

It was the next morning, after we had decided whose turn it was to make the tea, that I discovered when I went to switch on the kettle that we did not have any electricity. By the tone of the grunts that emanated from my beloved, anyone would think I had had the power switched off deliberately.

It was no doubt due to the bump in the night.

'I suppose I had better investigate,' declared the almighty from his bed, 'there's just no peace for some of us.'

We dressed quickly, went downstairs, opened the front door and stepped outside. I am not quite sure what we expected to find but, we both stopped dead in our tracks and gasped. The whole of the front field was covered with pieces of some white substance. We could not comprehend what the white phenomenon was – in fact it was strips of pure white wood. Those closest to the house were the largest whilst those furthest away were the size of matchsticks. By this time we had reached the middle of the field, still somewhat dazed and baffled by what we could see. Where had the wood come from?

In unison we both suddenly turned to face the house. I remember feeling almost frightened to look as if something terrible had happened. It was then that we saw the beautiful old oak tree that stood only twenty yards from the house had been split in two as if struck by a giant axe. Only one half of the tree remained.

It had obviously been struck by lightning; the massive explosion as the tremendous power of electricity earthed itself through the two-hundred-year-old oak had wakened us and torn the tree asunder, scattering the timber like confetti around the field. The blast had completely flattened the grass for at least fifty yards in front of the tree as if it had been covered by a mighty river in full flood, though in actual fact we had had no rain at all. Barbed wire which ran from the tree to a post only three yards from the house had completely disappeared. It had melted, burning the hedge in a twelve inch strip for twenty yards, finishing in a small blob of metal like the end of a welding rod.

We discovered when we went back into the house that plugs had been blown out of their sockets and tiny little pieces of wallpaper torn off the walls and strewn over the floor. It was then that Willi appeared to see if we were all right. The whole village was without electricity, which did not upset our routine too much but meant that the cows had to be hand milked, an experience as new to them as the young men who milked them. Quite an exciting and awe-inspiring experience, plus of course some of our lovely new grass was flattened, not that it took too long to reach skywards again.

Our field was eventually ready for cutting the first week in July and as Willi had finished making his hay, his tractor, mower and tedder were, thankfully, readily available. Malcolm started cutting at five thirty in the morning. A beautiful clear day, not a cloud in sight, birds singing and the sun pushing its steady path to the midday height. Ideally it should have been cut about eleven o'clock when the sun had sipped away any lingering dew, but with the promise of good weather to come, by the weathermen and a shortage of hours on our part, we did not feel a couple of hours would make that much difference.

My task was to follow Malcolm with a wide wooden hay rake, so that when the blades of the mower stopped because of a build up of grass, or a mouse nest impinged on the point, or just uneven ground, to free the blades, and to pull the cut grass clear from the hedge whenever Malcolm turned the tractor ready for the blade to drop cleanly onto the new cut.

By half past eight the whole field had been cut and Malcolm was able to go to the factory, albeit half an hour late. We were fortunate that Ben Finch, the manager, was very understanding.

Our new lay produced a good heavy crop, so we left it for two days before turning it for the first time; we turned it again the third day and hoped that perhaps it would just about be ready to bale on the fourth day.

It rained the fourth day and continued to do so for the next five days without a break; then we had two dry days – the crop was turned followed by more rain. Then unbelievably, a clear spell. The grass dried and turned into hay; we turned it three times before moulding it into long rolls with a side rake, ready for baling at last. Unexpected freak torrential rain fell before the baler reached us. We spread the hay back over the field hopefully to dry yet another wet spell.

The 'hay' lay waterlogged for six weeks. It was of no value at all and was suffocating any new growth that wanted to reach above the sodden crop, so we were forced to clear the field and sadly had no option but to burn the lot completely. Not a success story, and we found ourselves buying in hay for the animals during the winter months.

The following summer I was not at all enthusiastic about trying our hand at haymaking again and was all for buying in hay for the winter months if necessary and letting the animals eat the grass all the year round. But Malcolm was determined. He cut the grass. I was allowed to turn it three times – by hand. Malcolm formed the dry grass/hay into long sausages; drove the borrowed baler himself and we made superb hay in six days …and had it all stacked neatly in the barn into the bargain. Perfect hay – all because it did not rain. Oh, the joys of farming.

In the autumn of 1962 Bradley was born, two weeks early. Not exactly an element, but certainly a force to be reckoned with – are not all children? It was the 8th of October, a beautiful, warm, sunny day. We decided that we would make the most of the last of the summer sun and took fishing rods down to the stream in our lower field. Whilst Malcolm and Leigh were trying their hand at fishing, Shelly and I searched the hedges for blackberries. As fast as I picked so Shelly ate the lovely ripe berries or squashed them all over her dress. After I had managed to acquire about five pounds we joined the fishermen – me to rest on a rug and guard my blackberries from probing fingers, Shelly to try her luck with a hook and line. In fact it was Leigh who caught his first fish; a lovely three-quarter-pound trout – the only catch of the day. He was so excited. He kept looking at it and touching the silky, silver sides of the little trout before declaring that he would keep it in a box by the side of his bed as he did not really want to eat this particular fish.

Thankfully we were able to persuade him that a dead fish, no matter how attractive, was not the ideal bedside companion.

That evening friends came to join us for supper, during which our latest expected baby decided to put in an appearance – with very little warning. We sat down for the meal at eight o'clock, left for the hospital at nine o'clock and, as fathers were still not encouraged to see the birth of their children, Malcolm returned to Fronlas to finish his supper with our guests, Bradley being born at ten o'clock. I wished that I could have gone home to join Malcolm and our friends. I was so excited with our latest arrival all seven pounds and five ounces of him.

I stayed in hospital for five days and went home to yet two more weeks of sunshine. That lovely warm autumn was to herald one of the worst winters this century. Living in the country, the impact of a bad winter is far worse than in town.

We had a gentle fall of snow over Christmas, which

was very pretty and delighted the children. It was in January that we had the real thing. It snowed really hard all one Tuesday; huge fluffy flakes the size of half crowns, piling on top of each other, inching their way up the side of the house. Malcolm came home early in case the roads became really bad. The snow continued to fall thick and fast throughout the night, and by ten o'clock was accompanied by a howling gale which caused incredible drifting, bringing down telephone and electricity wires all over the country. Thankfully our electricity supply was intact, probably due to the shelter given by the hills above and behind us.

The next morning the hedges, fields and roads had become one huge snow plain. The children were thrilled; I was alarmed. I suppose being a townie, the fact that in the country we were so far from a doctor should the children need one in an emergency, was never far from my mind and now there was not even a road to lead us to town.

Malcolm, as usual, was constructive. 'We shall have to dig a way through,' he declared. 'The farmers must get their milk to the factories and there are at least four farms behind us. The roads are bound to be cleared from the town outwards so, if we start this end, clearing a path wide enough for one vehicle to drive through, we will eventually meet.' He did not add the fact that we would probably be one of the last areas to be cleared by the council lorries, as we were so far off the main road.

'I'll go up to Willi and we'll get this stretch organised between us.'

Malcolm returned an hour later, during which time I gave the children their breakfast and bundled them into warm clothes because they wanted to join in the 'fun'.

Bradley was fed and tucked snugly in his pram, but had to be left in the warmth of the house. I donned my boots and jacket and was also ready for action.

Malcolm had Ben with him – one of Willi's stalwart workers. Ben did not like speaking English very much. It was far more natural for him to speak Welsh, not that he spoke very much anyway and very slowly when he did. He was far happier with children and they in turn adored him.

He had a military type moustache that had grown wild, tinged a ginger brown where the smoke from the strange cigarettes he made curled and warmed the coarse hair, and kindly blue eyes that never showed anger – a gentle, placid, countryman. Ben never hurried anywhere but would keep going from dawn to dusk at the same steady pace, as I was soon to discover for myself.

It was decided that Willi and his men would clear the snow as far as our gateway from his farm, whilst Malcolm and Ben cleared the snow from the road from our gateway to the chapel.

After shovelling snow for three yards, Malcolm said, 'Here you are, June, you can have a go, and as we can't get in touch with Carmarthen I think I'd better try and get there over the fields, so that we know exactly what's happening.' Although it was five miles by road, it would obviously be quicker by cutting across country. A wave of the hand, and Malcolm disappeared in the general direction of Carmarthen.

The children joined in the snow clearing with the spades they normally used on the beach on warmer days than today, but every bit of help was welcome, though it did not take them long to tire of spooning away the never-ending pile of snow; there was far more fun to be had from rolling, throwing and falling about in that pure white softness. Loud shrieks and shouts accompanied their crazy antics.

At the time I did not mind being left with the snow clearing; any plan that would give us access to civilisation was welcome. Thinking back, I know I was frightened when in 1947 we had a very bad winter. I lived in Chippenham, Wiltshire; the roads were soon cleared and I played in the snow like all the other children and did not experience any hardships at all, but I heard reports on the radio and read in the newspapers that birds were freezing to death literally on the trees and sheep were being buried alive in deep drifts, though miraculously some survived after as much as fourteen days without food. Cows were marooned considerable distances from their home farm, huge bales of hay being dropped to them by plane and many tons of food were also dropped to people living in small villages cut off for days by the abnormal weather conditions, especially in the north of Scotland.

I hoped fervently that this winter would not be the same. All these thoughts were going through my mind as Ben and I gradually inched a cutting towards the chapel, some five hundred yards away.

Malcolm had left us at 8.30, saying that he would be back by midday. We stopped once for a cup of coffee but soon hurried back to the job in hand. We certainly did not feel cold, the exercise more than kept out temperatures below freezing point. I was quite pleased when the children asked when we were going to have some lunch; I was beginning to feel my shovel was much heavier than when we first started our marathon task. Ben pulled a lovely silver Hunter watch from the depths of one of his pockets (I think it was his most treasured possession) and after some deliberation said he thought perhaps the children might be right.

We slipped and skidded our way back to the house to have some piping hot soup from the big, brown casserole pot that I tried to keep topped up during the winter months. Slices of cheese on toast with home-made chutney were followed by a slice of boiled cake. A soggy fruit take which strangely most people seemed to enjoy. It looked like a conventional fruit cake that had had the oven door opened halfway through the making, causing the fruit to sink to the bottom. A real fruit cake was never fully appreciated in our household. The times I cringed when Malcolm would offer the boiled cake to visitors saying, 'June always makes a good fruit cake.' I could see the women quite often look at the heavy fruit mixture with slightly raised eyebrows, but nothing was ever said and every crumb devoured. One of the perks of growing older is that you no longer worry what people think – there are far more worthy things to take one's time.

Finishing our meal with two cups of tea apiece, Ben and I were ready to start work again. The children elected to stay in the house and play, keeping an eye on Bradley – a placid baby, little trouble as long as he was well fed and watered.

There was no sign of Malcolm, but Ben said he was probably a passenger on a snow plough, making his way home the easy way. I hoped that he was right. The sky looked heavy with probably more snow to come; if we could once clear the road, hopefully the big machines would manage to keep them open. With this incentive, I set about my snow clearing with renewed vigour. It was nearly five o'clock, we were within ten yards of the chapel when suddenly we were hailed from the other side of the hedge by Malcolm.

I was so pleased that he was back safely, but where was the snow plough? I had become convinced that by the time we reached the chapel a snow plough would have got through to us. Malcolm slithered over the hedge and landed at our side.

'My goodness, you've done well,' he said, giving me a quick hug. 'Look, I'll finish this off with Ben, you go back to the house with the children and prepare some supper. The snow plough is on its way down from Peniel, I could see it from the big field at the crossroads.'

He took my shovel and started clearing away the snow for all he was worth – where did he get his energy? Even as we were speaking we could hear the big machine closing towards us. Strangely it was quite exciting; it took so little time and effort to eat its way through the deep snow to our cleared passage. The driver leaned out of the cab, looked at Malcolm, holding my shovel, looked at Ben with his and said: 'My goodness you two have done well. If everyone helped themselves a little bit we'd soon get the roads clear. Well, I must be off, we're working the machines non stop until we know all the main roads are passable and then hopefully we'll keep them that way.'

He slammed the cab door shut and drove the huge machine back to Peniel. It was in fact five days before he came back to clear the road properly from the chapel to Hafod and on to Whitemill. It was such a relief to know that the road was clear enough to make contact with the outside world. I couldn't help laughing to myself that after all my efforts it was Malcolm who had the credit with Ben for clearing our road – at least in the eyes of the snow plough driver. It was Ben who said, 'You've got a good worker there'.

Praise indeed from the quiet man; it was he who had really worked hard and steady throughout the day.

'I know,' said Malcolm, giving me a quick wink. It was not until the children were in bed that night that we had time to talk about the day's events and Malcolm was able to tell me that the reason he felt he must get to the dairy and Carmarthen was, first, his responsibility to us as a family and secondly, his duty to be at the factory at such a critical time, to help organise a system to enable the farmers to deliver their milk to the dairy and direct however many staff had managed to reach the factory into the processing of the milk. He could not be sure that Mr Finch would have managed to get through, as he lived in a village just outside Carmarthen and no doubt would be experiencing the same problems as ourselves. As it happened, the snow plough cleared a way through his village at ten o'clock in the morning.

All milk over that period was sent by train direct to London, with no cheese production taking place whatso-ever. It had taken Malcolm three and a half hours to reach the factory at Pensarn. He had worked non-stop until 3.30 in the afternoon without a break before Mr Finch told Malcolm that he had better make tracks for home in case the heavy skies dropped yet more snow.

He was able to follow the road where a snow plough had cleared the way almost to the top of Peniel but had then reached a dead end. He assumed a snow plough must be coming from the Pencader direction to open the road completely. He therefore had no choice but to take to the fields yet again. It took him an hour to cover barely a mile, stumbling along in Wellington boots through bottomless troughs of snow, lying down and rolling over the hedges as he had done in the morning, but now he was very tired, his clothes wet, and he was very cold. It was sheer relief that had enabled him to clear the last bit of snow to the chapel. It was not until many years later that Malcolm told me that at one stage he wondered whether he would ever reach home safely and clearly remembers the thought passing through his head, how easy it would be to stop and have a little rest, how easy to give in and pass on. Strong words from someone not given to wild dramatics.

The snow also gave us its fair share of pleasure; apart from the beautiful scenery, the wonder of trees absolutely laden with sparkling jewels on those lovely cloudless sunny days, there were the snow fights with the children and of course the sledging.

I remember one evening in particular, when, after two very clear frosty nights we decided that we should have a toboggan party. We telephoned a number of friends and suggested that we hold the party the next evening (as long as the weather remained the same), with everyone to bring something for supper and a sledge if they had one, plus any children who were old enough to join in the fun; this way it would mean a lot of fun for everyone with very little effort.

A crisp frost and a full moon heralded the arrival of our friends. Some had brought their children, others had left them with babysitters, all laden with boxes and baskets. Malcolm had made up a lovely warm punch which proved very popular – after a few glasses we were all quite happy to go outside and try out our sledging skills down the good long slope of our top field. We started from the well, which gave us about one hundred and fifty yards of uninterrupted 'flight' – that was how it felt, especially if you had been given a hefty push-start by one of the men. We would stagger back to the top, dragging our sledges, only to race down again at break-neck speeds.

The children thought it a great adventure to stay up so late and have such fun instead of going to bed at their normal time. After about an hour we thought it was time for some food, so back into the house for a good varied supper, laced with as varied a collection of drinks as you ever did see. By the end of the meal the children were beginning to feel sleepy, but instead of taking them home, the parents settled them down in various beds, settees, sleeping bags and carry cots and were ready to go again. We raced up and down that hillside, shrieking like children; sometimes two on a sledge, sometimes three or four. On our stomachs, on our backs some of the men even tried it standing, but they were not very good at that – crouching was all they could muster with any success. All this after having consumed yet more of Malcolm's hot punch that he had carried up the hill in large metal jugs. Honey and Cindy, our two Labradors, joined in the fun as well – racing after as many sledges as they could, whilst three of Honey's latest litter of puppies sat fatly on the well cover, watching all the crazy antics with amazement.

It was good fun and I'm sure that the neighbours who did not come must have heard the racket, although we must have been at least half a mile away, and wished that they had joined us. We enjoyed every minute, midnight or not.

The river Towey froze over completely that winter and because it is a tidal river, layer upon layer of ice formed as the tides came and went; huge sheets of ice would suddenly rear into the air as the fast incoming tidal water surged in under the frozen layers, searching for a way through on its journey up the valley. It was inevitable that flooding followed the melting ice and snow, but this was taken to record levels because of the torrential rain that fell – as much as four inches in one night. We were lucky at Peniel with no real hardship, but for the factory and people who lived close to it, it was quite a different matter, their houses having been built only a few feet from the bank of the river. Consequently when the river burst its banks, the factory found itself in several feet of water – the docking area where the lorries normally unloaded the full churns of milk, could not be seen.

Not that flooding was unusual, it had happened many times before, but this time the rising water level was watched with added anxiety. At eleven o'clock that particular night it was very apparent that the high water mark would be the highest yet, so it was decided that the six huge electric motors that were in the basement of the factory would have to be unbolted from their positions on the floor and suspended from the ceiling with steel cables. The business of hoisting them above the crucial flooding point was achieved by using a block and tackle. It took three hours and six men working flat out to carry out the manoeuvre, by which time the flood water was a foot deep and rising fast. Although the water flooded up to two feet through the office block, the remainder of the factory and its contents were safely housed on higher levels – over all, amazingly little damage was caused.

It was not the case for the small number of people who lived in houses that bordered the river banks. Although they too were used to the normal flooding of the Towey and, it seemed, quite content to carry their belongings up to their bedrooms almost yearly, whilst the river coursed through their homes to a level of two feet, this time their houses were to take record levels – the downstairs rooms being filled right to the ceilings. I could never understand why the people continued to live so close to the river; the insurance premiums must have been astronomical.

One last incident completed that twelve months of experiences with the elements. It was our wedding anniversary, the twenty-third of March; we had decided to have a special dinner at home that evening with a bottle of good wine and just relax. I fed the pigs early. I bathed and fed the children early. I laid the table, complete with candles and flowers; everything that could be done in the kitchen was done. I had dared Malcolm that morning not to be late home that night. He wasn't. He was home on time armed with a beautiful bouquet of flowers. Everything was perfect. Malcolm opened a bottle of our favourite wine and had just filled our glasses when the telephone rang.

'You stay there,' said Malcolm, 'I'll answer the phone and tell whoever it is, we're busy.' He was back almost immediately.

'I've got to go into Carmarthen at once. That was the fire brigade on the phone, apparently the factory is on fire. They have tried to contact Len but there is no reply, so, I'm afraid I shall have to go. We'll have our dinner later – let's make it a romantic midnight dinner,' he laughed. 'I shouldn't be too long, it just depends how bad things are.'

There was no point whatsoever in making a fuss, so off he went to Carmarthen. He returned home at ten minutes to midnight. The meal of course was ruined so, we had cheese on toast with a bottle of wine. A different way of celebrating one's anniversary, but then through the years we often seemed to be doing things different from the norm.

We had experienced fire, flood, lightning and blizzard; all that was missing was drought. The summer of sixty-three produced drought conditions, but who complained, even if we were hauling water, because the well had run dry – the whole countryside needed to dry out before the winter started anyway.

Chapter Ten

The following autumn we were walking along the banks of our stream, enjoying the last rays of sunshine before the onset of winter. We realised that the blackberries had come to an end and the trees were almost leafless, revealing the warm glow of hips and haw berries on the almost naked trees.

'Pity there's no watercress in our stream,' said Malcolm.

'I dare say that's because it flows too quickly,' I replied – not being too concerned as watercress was not one of my favourite foods.

'I wonder if there's any in David's field,' Malcolm mused. There's quite a damp patch halfway across his field which could be surface water draining down to the stream, or it might be a small spring. Anyway, let's go and have a look.'

We scrambled round the boundary hedge where it met the stream and strode purposefully towards the spot in question. Not only did we find that in fact a spring was the cause of the dampness, but it spread its fingers into quite a large delta so that it only trickled gently into the stream. Ideal conditions for watercress, as we could see. A huge, lush dark green carpet of cress covered an area about twenty feet square and more.

'To think all that lovely watercress has been growing so close to us and we didn't know,' said Malcolm. 'I don't suppose David would mind if we had some. Perhaps he doesn't realise that it's there. Anyway, I'll give him a ring and ask him.'

We picked a small bunch and wandered back over two fields to the house. That evening Malcolm telephoned David (the farmer who owned the fields adjoining ours) and asked him about the watercress. He told Malcolm that he never touched it and that we could have the lot as far as he was concerned. That was the signal that put Malcolm's 'ideas bank' into overdrive.

'There's so much watercress, far more than we could ever eat; I reckon we should try to find a market for it,' he declared whilst we sipped our evening coffee. 'You could telephone the local supermarket in the morning and see if they're interested; and then you could try all the greengrocers in town as well. The more it's picked, the thicker it grows, so we may as well make the most of the opportunity.'

The next morning found me dialling the telephone number to the largest store in town. It was engaged. I was quite relieved; at least it delayed my request as to whether they would like to buy our watercress. I was not at all keen to contact this large store that had recently opened in Carmarthen, I preferred to just be involved with the local small greengrocer. Consequently, I telephoned the owner of the small shop in King Street where I normally bought all my fruit and vegetables. 'Yes,' was the reply, after I had explained about the surplus of watercress coupled with a request to drop in a couple of dozen bunches on Friday. I then telephoned the fish merchant – he said he would also like two dozen bunches.

I now felt a little more confident about my watercress dealings so I again dialled the telephone number of the largest shop in Carmarthen and asked to be put through to the fruit and vegetable buyer. I was informed that there was no such person but I would be put through to the manager. A couple of clicks in my right ear then a voice…

'Good morning, can I help you?' I explained that we had a large supply of watercress growing locally and would he be interested in buying any for the store.

'Ah well,' said the voice, 'we don't in fact do any direct buying here; everything is decided at head office and we just sell whatever is sent.'

(Goody, goody, I thought to myself, I've been let off the hook, but at least I would be able to tell Malcolm that I had tried. I was really chicken hearted.)

'However,' he continued, 'I will contact the fruit and veg buyer at head office and ask him if he would like to consider you as a supplier. Let me have your telephone number and I will ring you back.' I was obviously not off the hook yet. I did not hear from the store for two days and thought that they had either forgotten or were just not interested. No such luck – for on Thursday afternoon I had a telephone call from the local manager saying that he would like just one hundred bunches of cress delivered by eight o'clock on Friday morning – the next day in fact.

'Yes, of course,' I replied, trying to sound as if one hundred bunches would be no trouble at all. 'I'll make sure the cress is there on time, and thank you for the order.' I put the phone down and sat down. What had I let myself in for? If I could pick and bunch the watercress in time, for I had no idea really how long it would take to carry out that part of the operation, Malcolm could deliver the order on his way to the factory in the morning, so that would work out quite well. Next thing was rubber bands; I only had about fifty, so I rang Malcolm and asked him to buy some on his way home that evening. As it was now three o'clock I thought I had better hurry down to the cress bed to make sure that enough was picked before the light went, otherwise it would be dark and I would find myself picking water weed instead of watercress – they are not dissimilar.

Armed with two large polythene sacks and a pair of rubber gloves I hurried across the fields to the cress patch. It only took about half an hour to pick and fill the two bags which I hoped would be enough to make up one hundred bunches. I carried the cress back to the house and tipped the lot into the bath and turned on the water until it reached a depth of six inches. I thought that if I divided the cress in half and roughly made fifty bunches with one heap I would know whether I would have enough to make up the one hundred bunches by the time Malcolm came home with some more rubber bands.

It was quite fiddly picking out the pieces, keeping them fairly even and not end up with a bath full of leaves. It took me nearly an hour to make up fifty-four bunches, trim the ends and pack into some shallow boxes that I found in the garage. No doubt I would become quicker with more practice. I was not too sure that I really wanted any more practice. Malcolm came home that evening with a huge bag of rubber bands – it made me feel quite weak just looking at them knowing how many bunches of cress they could encircle.

'That should last you for a while,' he laughed as he dropped them on the kitchen table. 'How have you been getting on with the cress anyway?' I showed him the two full boxes of bunched cress laid in neat rows. 'Yes, they look fine, but I think they should stand in water until the morning and we can pop them into the boxes just before I leave. The cress will keep fresher that way.'

I agreed and returned the bunches to the bath, pushing the loose watercress to one end, and stood the fifty-four bunches in the relatively clear water. Once the children had gone to bed (no bath tonight), I bunched the remainder of our first order, threw out the scraps to the pigs, then typed out an invoice ready for Malcolm to hand over with the cress in the morning.

The following evening I could hardly wait for Malcolm to walk through the door before asking what had happened when he delivered our first consignment.

'What did they say and did they want any more?' I asked excitedly.

'Well, nothing really happened. I drove round to the Goods In entrance, a tall spotty lad came out of a little office, took the four boxes from me and asked for a delivery note, so I gave him the invoice, he nodded his head and disappeared through two self-closing doors, and that was it. I suppose if they want any more they'll ring, and I dare say we'll be paid at the end of the month,' he finished.

It seemed rather an anticlimax; in fact, it was the lull before the storm. The following Tuesday morning the telephone rang – it was the manager of the store.

'Ah, good morning,' says he. 'Thank you very much for the watercress last week. Actually, one of our quality controllers happened to be down on Friday and saw your cress delivery, in fact he was very pleased with the quality of the cress and that's why I'm ringing. We would like to increase our order to two hundred and fifty bunches (I gulped and felt quite sick) and...' he continued, 'our

Swansea branch would like two hundred and fifty as well. If you would bring the complete order into us in Carmarthen, we'll deliver the Swansea order ourselves. Thank you, Mrs Baker.' The telephone was put down and I... sat down.

Five hundred bunches: I obviously had to start picking and bunching pretty quickly; it was no good sitting around thinking about it, that only made it worse. So down to the cress field, this time with four polythene sacks which were twice the size of the ones I had used previously. My rubber gloves were invaluable but even so my hands became so very cold as I picked the cress from the ice-cold water. Unfortunately I could not wear gloves when bunching the cress as I could not seem to get the rubber bands round the ends of the stems without entangling some part of the glove in with the cress.

I dare say the reason for this was because the gloves were a little on the big side so that I could shake them off easily. The whole day was taken up with picking and bunching but the cress bed still stood lush, green and plentiful.

The next morning Malcolm again delivered the goods to the same spotty youth.

'Nice cress,' he apparently muttered before disappearing through the swing doors.

'I feel more like a porter than he does,' Malcolm complained.

'And I wish I had fairies at the bottom of the garden to help me pick the wretched stuff,' I complained back.

All was quiet for the rest of the week but Tuesday was on the horizon and coming closer. I hardly slept at all on Monday night and just could not seem to organise myself at all after breakfast Tuesday morning. I was just waiting for the dreaded telephone call. It came at half past ten.

'Good morning, Mrs Baker. Your local store here,' said a cheery voice. 'Lovely day isn't it?' He did not wait for my reply. 'Same as last week, please. Thank you.' There was a click as he put the telephone down and he was gone. It was as if my starter motor had been put into the fast forward position. I was galvanised into action; grabbing bags and gloves I made for the cress bed and carried out a repeat performance of the previous week which was to be repeated yet again the following week.

On the next Monday afternoon, the telephone rang. It was the manager of the Swansea branch of the company.

'Good afternoon, I understand you're the supplier of watercress to the Carmarthen branch and ourselves. We would like to make our order up to one thousand bunches this week and we will then send half of the order to our Cardiff store. No doubt the Carmarthen office will ring you tomorrow with their order but we felt it only fair to give you a little more notice as it is quite a substantial increase on our previous orders. I trust this will not present any difficulties?' he finished.

To say I was in a state of shock would have been the understatement of the year; I was beginning to think that half the population of Wales had suddenly become watercress addicts.

'There shouldn't be any problems,' I heard myself saying, but the heavy frosts we had had over the weekend were nagging at the back of my mind. I knew that I should have checked the state of the cress but I had been lazy and put it off. 'I will telephone you within the hour if I find that we can't manage the thousand bunches.'

I put the telephone down; I had a peculiar feeling that the cress would not be up to its normal standard. I pulled my anorak from its resting place; kicked off my slippers; thrust my feet into my Wellingtons and raced down to the field. How I wished that I had checked the cress beds but, whatever state it was in, was out of my control. However, I was not prepared for the sight that met my eyes. David's cows were in the cress field and it looked as if they had held a rock and roll competition right on top of the watercress. It was completely destroyed. I do not think there were ten whole stems left, let alone one thousand, two hundred and fifty bunches.

What on earth was I going to say to the store manager? I splashed through and round the trampled bed but it did not make any difference. The cress was finished and that was it. I turned and slowly made my way back to the house. In fact, it did not take many steps before the full realisation of what had happened really dawned. I was free. Free of dreading Tuesdays. Free of picking and bunching freezing cold vegetable matter. My bath was now free, seven days a week instead of only two. I felt quite delirious by the time I joyfully kicked off my boots in the porch.

I telephoned the Cardiff store first and explained what had happened to the manager. He thought it was a huge joke and did not seem at all concerned and just asked if I would let him know when I was back in business.

The Carmarthen manager was equally affable and merely said, 'Oh well, that's life,' thanked me for my service and hoped that we would be able to do business together again sometime in the future. Thinking about the state of the cress bed, I knew that no more business would be done that year; in fact, the cress bed was never so productive again.

In fact in thirty years Malcolm and I never came

across a bed of cress that equalled the one in David's field (thank goodness)!

A few years later legislation was brought into the growing and cultivation of watercress – concrete beds, running chlorinated water and inspectors to make sure the crop was grown in practically sterile conditions. I suppose this is progress but there is no better flavoured watercress than the wild variety – bugs and all.

Chapter Eleven

We had lived in the cottage Fronlas for about seven years, produced three children, organised pigs into a fairly good production line and fattening system; seemed to have settled on an average of twenty-two cats (one tame, twenty-one wild); taught our Labrador to 'sit, stay and heel' (can the normal family Labrador do anything else?) and, managed to stop our black and white collie rounding up the next-door neighbour's cows; holding them in a tight group in a corner of the field, and nipping noses or heels if they dared to step or nibble a single blade of grass over the imaginary boundary she had marked out.

Even the bees seemed to have become resigned to the fact that they were here to produce honey and make happy humming noises and not to terrorise the family during the summer months.

Leigh and Shelly had just about settled down at school, though that first day that I took Leigh into school is a day I will never forget (does any mother?). We were met by the infants' teacher, Miss Thomas; a plump, motherly soul with gleaming chestnut hair, kind dark eyes and a very happy, warm smile.

'Well, and who do we have here this morning?' she beamed. I held Leigh by one hand and Shelly by the other. I gently pulled Leigh forward and said, 'This is Leigh and he would like to start school.'

Leigh quickly assured Miss Thomas with a well aimed

kick to her shin that he did not and Shelly started bawling that she did.

'Don't worry at all,' Miss Thomas said patting me on
the shoulder as if I were one of her small charges, 'you'd
be surprised at the number of little angels who arrive at
the school gates only to turn into roaring demons as soon
as they're through them. If you would like to leave Leigh
with me I'm sure he'll be his normal self as soon as
you're out of sight.'

I did think that she was being rather optimistic, however, I said a quick goodbye to my roaring demon and left
him with one hand held firmly by Miss Thomas, the
other hanging onto a coat peg, kicking out with his new
school shoes in all directions. I dragged my bawling
daughter back to the car to join her younger, six-month-
old bawling brother (who wanted his breakfast) and
assured her that perhaps she could start school next term.
But I could not resist creeping back alone to peep
through the classroom window to see if all was well. I
could hardly believe my eyes; all the children were sitting
quietly on their little chairs, listening intently to Miss
Thomas' every word, not a single tear in sight, and there
had been quite a number of howling demons presenting
themselves at school for the first time that morning.

I returned to the car and drove home. We were very
lucky as Shelly was in fact able to start school a term
earlier than we had expected, which certainly made
things much easier. Yes, our routine was definitely
settling down. I now know this is a danger sign (where
Malcolm is concerned, that is).

One evening after dinner when the children had been
scrubbed clean, fed, watered and bedded down (as had
the pigs), we were sitting by the fire, a glass of our own

special mead in our hands when Malcolm said very quietly, 'I think we can now afford to look for a place of our own. Nothing spectacular – a house that possibly needs modernising, with about ten acres and a few outbuildings so that we can carry on with the pigs. What do you think?'

'It'll probably take all our savings,' I ventured, wondering what else his bombshell would evoke.

'Yes, but at least it would be ours and something we can improve and hopefully increase in value.' I knew that he was right, though I didn't relish the hunt. Back to translating the estate agents' half truths, at the right price; the normal dozen or so places that you drive straight past without even bothering to go inside; the other dozen you do go inside just in case it might be suitable and that's after you've managed to find the property in the first place after being given the most awful directions (I am sorry to say that we found a lot of people do not know left from right).

We were often told to go straight down the road, take the second turning on the right – at the same time indicating with their left hand to turn left. But when questioned, people would always say 'oh yes, I always mean the opposite.' We've tried it many times, in many towns and now know that one must substitute left for right and right for left, perhaps a speciality of west Wales.

No matter how many properties we looked at, none seemed to compare with our comfortable Fronlas. It was a pity that we were unable to buy it, but the trustees would not agree to sell. He who lived the longest would inherit the property – there were a couple of young trustees who, with good health, would keep the property off the market for many years to come.

We loved Fronlas despite the fact that the pigsties adjoined the house; that we'd had to cover the kitchen walls with cardboard then wallpaper over them to make it cosier (it was the only way to camouflage the white washed stones as we were not allowed to alter anything in the house at all.

I could never understand why, as surely anything would improve the value of the house; there were no objections to our installing electricity or bringing in the water supply at our expense. The well worked beautifully, the only time we had problems was when there was a particularly hard frost and the alkathene pipe which bridged a two feet gap from the field bank to the house, froze solid. The pipe had been very well insulated, but somehow we just could not keep the water from freezing as it entered the thick stone walls of the kitchen, so we always had to make sure that we had filled the kettle before we went to bed so that we could boil the water and defrost the pipe outside first thing in the morning, before we had a cup of tea.

Fronlas was a light, airy, sunny house and I suppose because it was our first real home it meant that much more to us, so when we did move, the new house (wherever it was) would have to have all the right prospects. One property that had potential came in the shape of a house and seven acres called Waunffordd, near the village of Llanstephan. Four rooms downstairs, which included the kitchen-cum-dairy-cum-store; four large double bedrooms, one single bedroom and a box room. No water, no bathroom and no loo.

I couldn't believe it – the cows in the cowshed across the yard had water bowls which filled automatically, whereas all the water for the house had to be carried across the yard manually. The only loo was a wooden two-seater, across the yard in what had been the vegetable garden – straddling the ever convenient stream. But… there was electricity.

The field in front of the house was about four feet high in stinging nettles and thistles. 'A sign of good land,' Malcolm assured me. I must say the other two fields certainly looked much healthier than the land at Fronlas despite all the fertiliser and attention it had been given in the shape of drainage trenches, weed killer and extra seed. Waunffordd had all the points that we were looking for – basically a sound family house but screaming out for modernisation in every direction (which should help to keep the price down); only five miles from Carmarthen and the factory; good land and buildings for the livestock; a school and beach just two miles down the road at Llanstephan. It was ideal. The only drawback was the fact that Waunffordd was for sale by auction – we would have to hope that luck was with us on the night of the auction.

We discussed our ceiling price for hours and the tactics, if any, we could use; it is so easy to become carried away at an auction. Looking back, it is strange that it just did not occur to us to even think of borrowing any money to back our savings to ensure that we could pay for the house if the final price was more than we had saved. Nothing was said between us, we both naturally assumed if we had not saved enough to pay the asking price, we would have to save some more money until we could.

We waited impatiently for the evening of the 30th July, some two weeks away – not telling a soul of our hopeful intentions.

During that time we discussed in detail how we could transform Waunffordd into a really interesting and spacious family home. It was a large square house; two large rooms in the front, either side of the front door, both eighteen feet square, and two rooms at the back of the house about the same size. The wall between two of the rooms could be possibly taken down, thus making a large spacious lounge running from the front to the back of the house; the other front room would make an ideal dining room and the store-cum-dairy, the remaining area, a good-sized kitchen and cloakroom.

Upstairs, the four large bedrooms could stay the same, the small single room could be converted into a bath-room, and the box room over the front door could be made into a sun room opening onto a balcony (to be constructed) that would give lovely views down to the river Towey. That was all fairly basic, according to Malcolm. The house would have to be re-plumbed; central heating installed; walls re-plastered and one taken down; completely rewired throughout; the whole of the outside would have to chipped off as the rendering was loose and just hanging in large blisters in many places, which held dampness into the walls; then of course the whole lot would have to be re-rendered and either painted or given a tyrolean finish (a new method of spraying walls) with a mixture of fairly liquid cement from a hand held box, turning the handle on the side as quickly as you could to obtain an even covering of the wall. A colour of one's choice could be added, but usually it was cream or white. New windows would have to be fitted all round as the existing ones were in very bad condition and were far too small anyway.

Then of course a garden would need to be formed to

set off the whole property, which initially would mean removing the hideous red brick wall which stood in front of the house only five feet from the front door, making an entrance drive and converting the field of stinging nettles into lawn, shrubs and flower beds.

The only thing the house did not need was a new roof; it was good, strong and sound, but there was an awful lot of work to be done. Would we be taking on too much (assuming we managed to outbid everyone else)? Malcolm seemed confident that we could cope with all the work 'and if we can't, we'll call in the experts, so there's no problem,' – there was no answer to that one.

We could not help wondering how many other idiots there were in the Carmarthen area who were hoping to buy Waunffordd at the same price, or even worse, a higher price than we were.

The sale was due to start at six o'clock – we arranged for someone to look after the children and arrived at the sale rooms at a quarter to six (we did not want to be seen as being too keen and possibly prospective buyers. We need not have bothered; to our consternation the room looked full of them).

We managed to find two empty chairs at the end of a row, two thirds of the way back from the auctioneer's table.

'This will do nicely,' Malcolm murmured, 'we should hopefully be able to see who is doing the bidding from here.' We settled down in our chairs and started looking at the people around us; some faces we knew and wondered why they were at the sale (no doubt they thought the same about us), but very many others we had never seen. My heart sank. I began to think that we did not have much of a chance after all.

Malcolm obviously sensed my thoughts, for he whispered, 'If we get it, we'll be lucky – if we don't, we'll save some more money and try again.'

Further talk was stopped by the auctioneer's gavel being struck on the table, twice. 'We are gathered here this evening,' he said (it sounded more like the start of a sermon than a sale, but perhaps we were about to learn a lesson) 'to dispose of the property known as Waunffordd in the parish of Llangain. This property is sold freehold together with seven acres of good pasture land. Make no mistake, ladies and gentlemen, it is to be sold this evening on behalf of the trustees of the property, and no doubt you will have satisfied yourselves on the questions of boundaries, etc.'

He droned on for what seemed ages, telling us things that we already knew; in fact, it was only five minutes before he said, 'Right now, who would like to open the bidding on tonight's sale?'

Silence from the crowd, but I was sure my heartbeat must have been quite audible. In my innocence I thought perhaps for one crazy moment no one other than ourselves was interested, but eventually a grunt came from the back of the hall.

'Ah,' said the auctioneer, 'we have a bid; somewhat low but no doubt we can build on it.' He obviously was able to translate the grunt into sterling.

A voice from just in front and slightly to one side of us said, 'Add £250 to it.'

'I'll take that as your bid, sir,' said the auctioneer, writing on the pad in front of him. After a long pause the grunter from the back of the hall mumbled, 'Top it up.' The slow bidding between the two came to a halt after four more bids.

Then Malcolm nodded his head. I was sure the auctioneer would not have noticed such a slight movement, but he had.

'Ah, new blood,' he said almost with relish. Another long pause then the big man just in front of us, slowly nodded his head (at least we had identified the enemy).

Malcolm straight away nodded again. 'I see we have a contest on our hands,' said the auctioneer, this time with obvious glee. I could hardly bear to look up, I could not breathe properly and my heart was beating in double time. Another long pause and then another slow, deliberate nod from the big man in front – almost daring us to bid again. Malcolm retaliated with a quick, sharp nod. Would the big man reply? We had reached our limit. A long, long silence. Then the auctioneer said loudly and clearly, 'I am offering you Waunffordd for the last time. Are there any further bids?'

My head was lower than ever, though my eyes were firmly fixed on the big man.

'Going once. Going twice,' then… bang, the gavel came down on the table with a thunderous thud. Waunffordd was ours. Malcolm gave my hand a quick squeeze as the auctioneer said, 'Would the purchasers please come to the table so that we can arrange the legalities?'

Nobody moved very much. People were standing up but no one seemed actually to leave the room. I now know that the majority of people attending a house sale normally stay until they have identified the buyers. This more so in country districts – I suppose they want to know who the new neighbours will be.

I was then aware of the big man making his way towards us. 'Congratulations,' he said, extending a hand to Malcolm. 'I would have liked Waunffordd for myself but it was not to be. You've certainly got some work to do but it's a good solid house. I'll no doubt be seeing more of you, I live further up the hill in Llangain.'

We wrote our signatures on about a dozen pieces of paper, gave a cheque for ten per cent of the purchase price, were told completion date would be on the 30th August and left the sale room in a bit of a daze. In thirty minutes or less, we had disposed of all our savings except for twenty pounds and landed ourselves with an enormous workload. But we now owned our very own house the incentive was there.

'Let's hope the price of pork goes up pretty quick,' laughed Malcolm as we drove back to Fronlas. It did – but it always used to in the autumn anyway.

We could hardly wait for the 30th August to arrive when we could collect the keys from the solicitors and really set our plans for Waunffordd in motion.

We had been lucky enough to be allowed to cut the stinging nettles, but not a stone could be put out of place or our feet be allowed to cross the threshold until completion date. Malcolm had first cut the nettles with a big Allan scythe, and a section of the field down to the road that we had decided we would turn into a garden. As soon as he had cut the high nettles and long grass I was allowed to rake it into heaps – it looked as if we were hay making. For a week it looked like wheat stubble, but it gradually softened as it grew longer; it was then cut again with an old drum mower and by completion day, it really was beginning to look like a lawn. As Malcolm explained, the field was old permanent pasture with so much clover, meadow fescues and perennial rye grass that it almost had no option but to turn itself into a green carpet.

'We'll dig over the area we want to turn into flower beds in October so that the soil will have time to break down during the winter months and be just right for planting next spring.'

We planned to stay in Fronlas for the winter, which would give us six months to sort out the inside of Waunffordd and move in the following spring; hopefully in March when it would be somewhere near complete, thus giving us the summer to concentrate on the outside.

The 30th August at last dawned but it would be evening before we could actually let ourselves into the house. The children had just started back to school and Malcolm was of course at the dairy. However, I fed the pigs a little earlier than usual – not that they minded in the least; they, like all pigs, were always ready for food and squealed their heads off in anticipation as soon as I opened the pigsty door.

Feeding the pigs was like running an obstacle race; once you had your bucket full of barley meal, you had to run the length of each trough, emptying the meal evenly as you went, before any of the pigs managed to reach the trough before you and trip you up in the process. The thought of a pen load of pigs (usually about twenty in number) trampling over you is enough incentive to keep you soundly on your feet.

Once they had been fed and the floors given a quick hose and brush down, I left them to finish their meal in relative peace. I packed a picnic tea, then drove into Carmarthen, picked up the children from school, collected the keys for Waunffordd from the solicitors, then went down to the dairy in the hope that Malcolm would be finishing on time. Surprise, surprise, he was actually waiting for us, an unknown phenomenon.

We arrived at the house with two keys, both of the mortise lock variety. We tried the front door first; the key turned in the lock but the door was obviously bolted from the inside. So, we traipsed round to the back door and with a slow turn of the key and a whispered 'open sesame', the bottle green door swung open.

Leigh and Shelly pushed past us into the cool house, anxious to see their new home. We were anxious too but wanted to take it in a little slower; in fact, we were still in what we hoped would be the lower half of the lounge when the two children raced in, having completed a quick tour of the house and declared the fact that there were no beds or bathroom; they did not like any of the wallpaper; could they play outside and when was tea?

Yes they could play outside and we would have tea in about ten minutes. 'Will it be a short ten minutes or a long ten minutes?' asked Shelly, who was always ready for her meals.

Before either of us could answer, Bradley, who had been content up to this stage just to sit in the middle of the room (he was nearly a year old and neither talked, walked or crawled anywhere) picked up the vibes that food could be in the offing and started banging on the floor with his favourite spoon, from which he was seldom parted (apparently he was quite normal, just lazy).

'Perhaps if we have tea now the three of them will probably be happier to play for a while,' I suggested. So back outside we went, deciding to have our picnic on the front lawn, well, it would be a lawn eventually. Fortunately Bradley seemed to be on the sleepy side after his meal and curled up on the blanket and went fast asleep. Meanwhile, Leigh and Shelly had found a swinging tyre in the Dutch barn and were quite happy to explore generally. The outbuildings were apparently far more interesting then the house. We returned to the 'lounge', with Malcolm carrying a crowbar which he had taken from the back of the Mini van.

'I just want to see exactly what this wall is made of,' he said as he gently eased the thin edge of the crowbar under the wallpaper and into the plaster. Within a few minutes had had removed about two square feet of plaster, revealing neat rows of red bricks.

'Um, just a little bit more,' he mumbled, followed by a triumphant 'Ha: Just as I thought, brick and timber frame,' – then as if for good measure, he pushed three of the bricks straight through the wall into the adjoining room.

I must admit that I was somewhat alarmed; having spent all our savings on this house I did feel that perhaps Malcolm should be exploring with a little more caution – I had visions of us having to rebuild the whole place. However, to keep me quiet (and I suspect confirm for himself) he did fetch the ladder and check the roof supports and surrounding masonry, confirming the wall was not a load-bearing wall.

'That's a good thing,' he smiled, 'we just knock down the whole wall and we'll have a lovely, large lounge.'

'With two fireplaces,' I added. We inspected both of them. The one in the front room of the house was a Victorian glazed tile affair – this had obviously been the 'best room'. The other fireplace was a black range complete with swinging kettle hobs – apparently the old kitchen, although there was no water or electricity. Thankfully, it would not be too much of a problem to install these facilities as both were readily available across the yard in the cowstall.

'Which fireplace do we keep and what do we do with the one we don't want to keep?' I asked. Neither were particularly interesting or inspiring in their present state. The Victorian fireplace just occupied a boring space on a plain wall, whereas the black range lived in its own dark closeted hole.

Malcolm again reached for the crowbar and started thumping the wall surrounding the old oven.

'It won't be much of a problem pulling that old thing out and once the whole lot is cleared, we would have quite a decent sized cavity and could easily make it big enough to stand in if we were to take away the existing stone lintel and replace it with a nice timber one.'

There was a long thoughtful pause. 'But I think the new lintel should be slightly higher,' he added.

We discussed the merits of turning the recess into an inglenook fireplace, but decided against this idea as the fire would be too far back and not in a central position for such a large room – approximately thirty feet by fifteen feet by the time we removed the dividing wall. We then reached the decision that a feature of some sort could be made of the old range area, but exactly what we were not too sure. Some thinking was to be done in that direction, but we did decide that the working fireplace would be the Victorian one, but with an interesting feature built into the structure.

Next the old cheese store and pig salting room came under scrutiny as this was to be the kitchen. Again, windows were to be installed as at the moment there were only wooden shuttered grilles that let any light into this north-facing room. A hatch into the adjoining dining room would be useful as it was quite a long haul down the passage to the dining-room door. A new floor would have to be laid after the removal of the very badly cracked, flaking stone slabs – a mammoth task in itself. Some of the slabs were six inches deep by over three feet in length. Unfortunately, we could not lay a new floor on top of the old slabs as the levels would be completely wrong. Obviously water would have to be plumbed in, kitchen units installed and we thought a breakfast bar would be useful, especially where the children were concerned.

We decided to turn the small box room into a sun room, changing the small window for a full length door which would lead onto a balcony to be constructed above the porch (which also would have to be built) and front door. The smallest bedroom would convert nicely into a bathroom and basically, that was it – the rest of the house just needed re-plumbing, rewiring, central heating installed, new windows in every room and complete redecoration.

Then of course there was the outside of the house to be considered. The old rendering, which had covered the walls for so many years, was cracked and crumbling and would have to be completely removed from the original stonework. Unfortunately, the stonework was not good enough to leave revealed and would require rendering with cement and giving an attractive finish.

The cleaning of the stone is called 'chipping out', a long laborious job, using a small pointed hammer, tapping, thumping and banging round each stone, removing every single loose particle so that the cement would hold when it was smoothed onto the walls. I knew instinctively who would land the position of Chief Stone Chipper – and I wasn't wrong. Unfortunately in 1964 the mechanical tool which is used today had not been invented. Unlike the house, the outbuildings were in very good condition; light and airy, running water with taps everywhere and electricity; possibly all that was needed was a fresh coat of whitewash.

By now the children were beginning to get restless so we decided it was time to make tracks for home – we certainly had plenty to think about. Llangain was only five miles from Carmarthen and Fronlas was only a further five miles so the journey only took about twenty minutes – a trip to be made many, many times before we were able to move into our modernised property.

We decided that we would work on Waunffordd through the winter months, concentrating totally on the inside of the house in the hope that we would have it habitable and ready for us to move into in the spring; then with the summer in front of us we could transform the outside (the same programme that we used on Fronlas and repeated again in the years to come).

I spent many days over at the house during the autumn months just with Bradley whilst Leigh and Shelly were at school; I would finish in time to pick them up and take them home for tea. Malcolm would sometimes join us for a meal in the evening but more often than not he would go straight to Waunffordd from the factory and work until ten o'clock at night before coming home cold, tired and hungry.

I particularly remember one cold, foggy November evening when he came in looking absolutely shattered although it was only half past eight – it was not so much as a tired look as the slightly dejected hang to his shoulders.

'What on earth is the matter?' I asked anxiously.'

'You obviously haven't heard the news,' he said sombrely. 'President John Kennedy has been assassinated in Dallas, and somehow after hearing that, I just couldn't seem to settle down to doing any more work, so I thought I may as well come on home.'

I just could not believe it – the shock tremors covered the world. It was the first of many assassinations carried out on world leaders that affected the world and not just the particular country where the crime had been committed. To follow that atrocity was the shooting of Robert Kennedy, and that of Martin Luther King; the kidnapping of President Lumumba of the Belgian Congo (his body was never found); then in later years, President Sadat of Egypt, mown down by his own soldiers; Mrs Indira Ghandi murdered by one of her own personal guards; and of course, attempts on our own Conservative leader Mrs Thatcher and some of her cabinet ministers when in 1985 a bomb, planted by the IRA in the party conference hotel, exploded, killing one person and injuring several others. Even the orderly country of Sweden was not to escape the violence, for their own president was assassinated in 1986.

We worked on through the winter months, me during the day, Malcolm in the evenings, and together at the weekend. The children loved the weekends, especially the food side; although we had an electricity supply for lights, we did not have cooking facilities, and consequently I heated soup, cooked eggs, bacon, sausages and anything else that would fit into a frying pan on a tiny primus stove that threw huge sheets of flame to the ceiling whenever I tried to light the wretched thing. I think this was due to the fact that I never seemed to be able to insert the pricker quick enough. Other times I would achieve clouds of evil-smelling paraffin. I hated that primus stove. We eventually went crazy and bought a new type of burner made by a company called GAZ. It was a blue container with a cooking ring on the top but most important of all a control knob on the side. Sheer bliss: How that company has progressed since 1964.

I spent many hours banging, gluing, pushing and screwing our kit-form kitchen units together. They were made of solid wood except for the worktop which was made of a new material called Formica. The doors and drawers I painted blue, which in the early sixties was the in colour for kitchens.

The new Marley plastic floor tiles in squares of yellow and white completed the colour scheme and were so easy to clean after the old type linoleum. By March our labours had paid off for we had completed enough of the house to enable us to move into our new abode. The fifteenth was set as Moving Day. Not for us a smart, nationwide, well-known company with men in smart uniforms to do the humping and carrying – but a tractor and trailer borrowed from Willi and our best friend to help us with the loading. Two good loads was all it took. We did not seem to own very much at all once it was all consolidated onto the trailer. Malcolm covered the bulging heap of possessions with a huge green tarpaulin and roped it securely to the ironwork; then almost as an afterthought, he pushed some odd bits of timber and a couple of doors between the rope and the tarpaulin. 'You never know when they might come in useful,' he said in answer to my question about old rubbish. It was not until many years later that I found out that it was illegal to move furniture with a tractor and trailer as it was not connected to agriculture – hence Malcolm's attempt to disguise the load. But in those days I do not think anyone would have really minded other than a certain bobby who always seemed to be after Malcolm's hide for some trivial reason or another; on the other hand he seemed to be after many peoples' hides and was not at all the most popular of people. He would have made a good traffic warden of the worse variety (not that we had traffic wardens in 1964). He would stand for hours, waiting to see if someone went over the time allowed on a parking limit, or wait behind bushes at halt signs to see if you actually stopped and if you did not stop he would practically commit suicide by leaping out in front of the car to take your name and address. Luckily for us old Richard was not to be seen that day.

It took Malcolm one and a half hours to travel to Waunffordd and one hour for the return journey, consequently the whole morning was taken up just moving furniture. A quick lunch and we started on the pigs. We were very fortunate here as Mr Lewis of Dany-graig Farm let us borrow his cattle trailer. Two good loads of pigs soon emptied the sties. Malcolm's brother did the pig delivery for us, which enabled Malcolm to load the furniture trailer one more time with tools, a saw horse, timber and all sorts of things that men treasure and women would throw away, though the opposite could be true as well, I suppose.

I drove to Waunffordd taking the children, all the bedding and anything else that did not manage to be squeezed in or onto the trailer. I arrived just as the second load of pigs were slipping and sliding down the ramp before scampering through the door of their new home, no doubt looking at once for the food troughs, which of course were empty. The journey no doubt had upset them a little and of course their normal routine was definitely disturbed, so, I decided to feed them straight away, which would certainly please them and help them to settle for the night, and of course it would be another job out of the way. It did not take long at all as the arrangement of the pens was so much better than at Fronlas, plus of course they did not need cleaning out afterwards. I gave them some straw, which they played with before making their bed for the night – snuffling through the barley stems and tossing them over their backs, perfectly happy.

Then I turned my attention to the children; a quick bowl of cereal and the promise of their favourite meal later. I decided beds were the next priority. The pile of sheets and blankets soon disappeared onto the waiting beds and the children were very helpful and attacked their own boxes and cases of clothes with great glee, pushing jumpers, shirts and blouses into cupboards and drawers in a race to see who could unpack the quickest. At least the bedrooms were beginning to look quite tidy, even if I was going to have a bit of a job locating the different clothes as and when they were wanted.

Malcolm arrived with the trailer and tractor, which he insisted on unloading straight away, most of it being thrown into a large store near the roadside which apparently was going to be his workshop. I was very pleased that it would not be my job to sort out that particular lot. Fortunately, the tractor and trailer did not have to be returned to Gwili until the next day so we decided that we had done quite enough and it was time to relax.

'Oh hell,' Malcolm suddenly exclaimed, 'the pigs; I'd better do them now, I'll certainly not feel like doing it after dinner.'

'Mummy's done it, Mummy's done it,' chanted the

children. Malcolm was just about all in, he was so pleased he did not have to rally once more. Everything is such an effort when you are really tired. It had been a very long day and driving the precariously loaded trailer must have been quite nerve-wracking. Somewhat revived after dinner, we read a couple of stories to Leigh and Shelly whilst Bradley watched and half listened from his high chair. It was his haven where he could see everyone and everything and, more importantly, from which direction his food was coming. Poor Bradley had not had much exercise that day as he had spent most of it either in the car, in his chair or in the swing we had rigged up in the kitchen doorway.

At seventeen months he still showed little inclination to crawl anywhere, let alone walk. Malcolm lifted him out of the chair and stood him by his side. Bradley could stand very well and did so for long periods but eventually would sit down with a soft thud on to the floor.

'Come on, old chap, it really is time you started to walk,' said Malcolm giving Bradley a gentle push. And he did. He walked the full length of the kitchen. At long last – we could hardly believe our eyes. Leigh and Shelly were as pleased as Bradley obviously was. He had reached the end of the kitchen before sitting down with a soft plop; he still had to learn how to do the turn but the delight on his little face was a joy to see.

On looking back I'm sure that he had made up his mind not to spend time crawling about the rubble and mess that we were making everywhere but wait until the place was fit to walk in and walk he did. There was no stopping him, except for field walking which he seemed to dislike intensely. He would stand and bellow like a rambunctious calf; he wanted to be carried, preferably on someone's shoulders so that he could see everything. But this was not to be encouraged and he would have to give in and walk or be left behind, which he hated even more.

It was lovely being in our own house at last, even though there were gaping holes round the window frames which could not be properly filled until the outside of the house was rendered.

'Fresh air is good for you,' my beloved assured me. Well, there was certainly plenty of it about. We worked solidly during those early summer months, inside if it was wet, outside if it was dry – we did not waste a single minute. Our efforts soon began to show; even the garden sported a brilliant display of annuals, dahlias, begonias and shrubs and was beginning to have a really good 'cared for' look. The well-mown lawn of nettles and thistles was superb.

We were really beginning to enjoy living in our first real home.

Chapter Twelve

Early one August afternoon Len Haines, a vet friend of ours, called in to see how we were coming on with our renovating. He knew Waunffordd very well having lived in the village of Llangain all his life until he left to do his veterinary training. His brother and parents still lived in the village but Len now lived in Carmarthen with his wife Fiona and their two children where he had his own veterinary practice.

After a tour round the 'site' (our home, in other words) of half-built wall, exposed ceilings and gaping holes that would eventually hold windows, Len suggested that we ought to take some time off and relax a little so… how about some light fishing? Malcolm and I exchanged quick glances; the rod and line sport was not for us, we had decided some time ago. Len translated the look between us very accurately.

'It's not sitting on a bank with a rod, hook and worm that I'm talking about, it's Wellington boots and buckets you'll be needing.' Our bewildered faces made him laugh heartily before explaining this new form of fishing. 'Certain families through the years have traditionally been given the right to use static nets for fishing in the river Towey. Though the tidal fishing area is in fact common land, access to the river is private, hence not many people fish the river this way. Basically, long stakes are driven into the river bed in a straight line and left there permanently, the nets are then fitted like a huge curtain at the low tide before you actually want your fish; nowadays most people use chicken wire and not the traditional rope nets. As the tide goes out the flounders, mud dabs or flat fish, call them what you like, all being bottom-feeders, are trapped in the base of the net. All you have to do is pick them up. The point is the net has been down for four tides; my parents and brothers have had all the fish that they need and it's my turn tonight. So I wondered if you'd like to share the catch with me, and in return give me a hand to take the nets down as they must not be left in position permanently or the fish not removed, otherwise a great many fish would die unnecessarily and of course the nets would fill up with all sorts of rubbish; the nets therefore are emptied religiously after each tide or removed. Normally the family only fishes during the month of August and pops any surplus into the deep freeze.'

'Surplus in the deep freeze?' I asked. 'Do you mean you catch more than enough for one or two meals?'

'Well, depends on the catch, but normally we do,' Len smiled.

'It's certainly different from any way we've heard of catching fish, and we could certainly do with a breather,' said Malcolm.

'Will it be all right to bring the children?' I asked.

'Yes, of course.'

'Will you be bringing Rachel and Andrew?'

'Might as well,' was the reply.

'In that case, ask Fiona to bring their pyjamas. Then, when we've finished fishing, the children can have some supper and go to bed here. I know Leigh and Shelly would love that and it would give us a chance to have a bite together as well and catch up on your activities. You could pick the children up in the morning or we could easily pop them into Carmarthen.'

It was arranged that Len, Fiona and their children would arrive at six o'clock that evening, which only gave us just over an hour and a half to feed the children, feed the pigs, feed ourselves and clean up our tools and some of the mess we had made during the day. We were ready with three minutes to spare.

We decided that we should each take our cars, then if the fishing took longer than was anticipated or if the children became overtired (I could not help thinking I might become fed up with fishing myself) at least Fiona and I could bring them back to Waunffordd.

We bundled our fishing gear into the back of the car – not that anyone would ever recognise it as such – consisting only of Wellington boots, a bucket, a couple of sticks and two empty fertiliser bags; that being all that we would need, our fisherman host assured us. The men and the two eldest boys went in one car; Fiona and myself with the two girls in the other.

Bradley joined us womenfolk as he had not yet reached the age of 'being with the men'. We left the house and drove towards Llanstephan for about a mile before turning left into a gateway.

'We normally drive across this field and leave the car in the bottom corner, which means that we don't have to hump the fish or the gear too far,' explained Fiona.

Or carry Bradley too far, I thought to myself. At twenty-two months he still showed little enthusiasm for walking. But there were some advantages to this laziness. I picked up his blanket and harness, knowing that he would be quite happy and safe to sit on his blanket for ages without moving as long as he could see someone, and if he did by any chance decide to move, it would not be more than twelve feet. We had adapted the walking harness that had been used by both Leigh and Shelly to take a length of dog chain from the back of the harness, with a tee bar fastened to the last link. This could then be pushed through a metal hoop which was pushed firmly into the ground, the six feet of chain gave him a good area of safe crawling. It was ideal if we were working in the fields, hedging or haymaking and, on the odd occasion, playing tennis. The tee bar was slipped through the wire surrounding the tennis court, with the result that whichever child was 'on the chain' could be seen by the parents and not come to any harm. The time we could use the system was very limited as it only covered the time children were happy to sit and play with toys or just crawl. My mother always maintained that as Bradley made the most use of it, he must be quite bright, as he had obviously worked out at a very early age that everything comes to he who waits – and of course it did.

We thought that it was a good system, though no doubt there would be many who would be horrified at the thought of basically chaining up a child, but the children were perfectly happy and it enabled us to be more relaxed in whatever job we were trying to do and of course they had more freedom than if they had been stuck in a pram or pushchair.

But now, it was time to try out this new-to-us method of fishing. We bumped slowly over the field to squeals of delight from the girls and came to a stop by a gap in the hedge in the corner. The children tumbled out of the cars and quickly put on their boots, ready for action straight away. How frustrating it must be for children to have to wait for their parents to climb so slowly out of the car, taking ages to put on their boots and spend so much time rummaging around in the boot of the car and never bringing anything interesting out of it, and not only that, having to endure the shouts of their parents 'don't go too far', 'come back here'. Worse still, 'you can help to carry something', all when there was so much to be seen just a hundred yards away.

Pushing our way through the hedge, carrying sticks, buckets, bags and Bradley, we made our way some two hundred yards across a sandy dune-like area which led to the high water mark of the river Towey. We could see straight away that the tide was already receding with about ten yards of muddy silt easing itself ever wider towards the sea.

'The timing couldn't be better,' said Len. 'You can just see the tops of the poles showing above the water' and he pointed where, some two hundred yards out, the fast ebbing tide was giving us a glimpse of our fishing ground.

The estuary of the river Towey at this point was about half a mile across and I knew by the time the tide had completely withdrawn, the river itself would be no wider than twenty yards. 'Well, what's the form?' asked Malcolm.

'Within half an hour the nets will be quite clear of the water and that's when we get to work,' said Len. 'Meanwhile, we'll just watch and see what's about.'

I settled Bradley on his blanket, put on his harness and anchored him firmly to the ground with the tee bar and hoop. I instructed Leigh and Shelly not to go in the muddy silt in case they became stuck or fell over in it and set myself ready to see anything and everything that was on the move.

'There! There!' Len shouted suddenly, pointing at the

appearing nets. I was just in time to see a searing flash of silver followed by a hefty splash in the water on the seaward side of the net.

'What sort of fish was that?' everyone wanted to know.

'A salmon bass,' came the knowledgeable answer. 'They come back down the river with the tide, feel the net in front of them and invariably will leap over it, though sometimes they'll work their way to the side and then become caught up in the decreasing circles of net at each end; you'll see what I mean once the tide has gone out completely. The fish that we're after tonight are the flats and flounders; they're bottom-feeders, grovelling in the mud on the river bed for mud worms, which are particularly plentiful at this time of the year.'

We saw two more salmon bass jump the net but then had to content ourselves with watching the ebbing tide and the appearance of the nets. After thirty-five minutes, the full thirty-inch depth of the chicken wire was fully exposed; a fact that had not escaped the notice of a dozen or so swooping seagulls, shouting their raucous call which, translated, would appear to announce that some easy fishing was available for they were being quickly joined by other screaming, hungry gulls – not that I could see any fish from where we were standing.

'Those gulls are the best guide as to when to make a move,' said Len. 'If you don't get out to the nets fairly quickly once they start gathering, they'll tear to pieces or carry away anything that may be trapped. I think probably the best plan will be for Malcolm and me to get straight out to the nets and start picking up, and you and Fiona come at your own pace because it's pretty heavy going and slippery through the mud. Bring a bucket each and we'll all take a stick.'

'To lean on,' I said brightly.

'No,' said Len, 'you'll need the stick to help you find the fish.' I must admit I was expecting the fish to be on the surface waiting to be popped into my bucket but I thought I had better not say anything, better to wait and see.

Len and Malcolm squelched off in the direction of the nets, Fiona and I went to follow, but not before again telling the children to stay on the bank. I soon found it no easy task to move forward at any speed; the river bed was very slippery and when I tried to lift one boot in front of the other, nothing happened whatsoever. The only way one could propel oneself along was either by skating along very slowly (feet drifting in all directions), or by lifting the heel of one boot, letting the air in under the sole, leaning heavily on the stick (despite what Len had said, it made an ideal prop) and heaving the boot free from the sucking silt, whilst at the same time pulling hard on the back of the boot with my free hand; the bucket and stick being tightly clutched in the other. It took a fair few minutes to get into a rhythm of forward movement.

Fiona did not appear to be making any faster headway than I was. It took us about eight minutes to cover the two hundred yards to the edge of the net, by which time the mud was within five inches of the top of our boots.

'How are you two men getting on?' we called in chorus to our menfolk who were bent double in the middle of the line of poles.

'Fine,' shouted Malcolm. 'There are plenty of fish, but it's very heavy going.'

'Well, in that case, we'll stay at this end,' I shouted.

We had found it bad enough reaching the net and we

had not even picked up a single fish as yet. It crossed my mind that if we did find some fish, it was not going to be any easier getting back with a bucket of fish to carry into the bargain. I looked at our fishing grounds; certainly not the traditional fishing layout one is accustomed to seeing, where fish and water share the same domain.

Fifteen poles had been driven into the tidal area in a straight line, covering approximately fifty yards running parallel to the bank. A continuous length of weathered chicken wire three feet wide had been secured to each pole with straw coloured binder twine, the last six inches of wire being buried in the silt, each end of the wire curtain finishing in three or four ever decreasing circles.

The technicalities of these observations were explained to me thus; weathered chicken wire is used because new wire would be bright and frighten the fish. The same reason applied to the natural coloured binder twine. The wire ran parallel with the river flow in the tidal area so that as the tide ebbed to the main stream of the river, the fish would be trapped against the wire. The wire was set in decreasing circles at each end to catch any fish that worked their way to the end of the wire curtain – had it not been curved into a circle, it would be easy for the fish to slip round the end, into free water.

Now to catch our fish. Easier said than done. I could not even see any fish, which was not a very good start. We stole a glance at the men; they were poking at the base of the net with their sticks, bending down for a couple of seconds, straightening up before starting their sticks back into action again.

They were obviously picking up fish. I pushed my stick tentatively into the soft, silky mud; a small grey fin broke from the surface.

'I've caught a fish! I've caught a fish!' I shouted excitedly. But I did not have a fish. I had only seen a fish. I dropped the stick in my excitement and started grubbing about in the murky, sandy slurry. I touched something firm and grabbed at it quickly, only to have my fish (for that was what it was) flip itself clear of my grabbing hands. My next attempt to catch my slippery customer carried a little more thought. I immersed both hands gently into the mud and carefully sifted through the silt until again I felt my fish. I managed to place a hand each side of the flat rubbery creature and pluck it clear of the sucking mud, only to have it slide through my fingers again, landing with a plop on the muddy surface. This time I pounced like a cat onto my prey; caught the fish firmly round the middle and dropped it quickly into my bucket. Success at last. After that first effort I was on a quick learning curve and other fish quickly followed each other into my yellow, plastic bucket. Within twenty minutes I had filled the bucket three quarters full, which I estimated to be about as much as I could manage to carry safely to the bank, hoping that I would not slip and fall in the mud and lose the lot.

Fiona had managed to land about the same number as myself, so we decided to make our way back together shouting our decision to the men. We made our way very, very slowly back to the bank and firm ground. The children gathered round us excitedly, to see what we had caught. Even Bradley, who had sat so passively on his blanket during all the activity, thumped his spoon on the ground as if in anticipation of all the fish dishes to come. Little fat fingers explored the buckets, feeling the mud-covered fish, exclaiming over the odd faces – some with heads turned to the left and some to the right and one in particular that looked remarkably like a well-known traffic warden. They really were extremely interesting creatures. It is an odd phenomenon that the eyes of these bottom-feeders do in fact vary, some fish looking to the left, others to the right.

Whilst we had been inspecting our haul, the men had made their way to us, their plastic sacks obviously holding far more fish than we had managed to catch. We really had been extremely lucky; between us we had unbelievably picked up about one hundredweight of fish. Malcolm and I had had no idea that the catch would be so great, or taken with such relatively little effort. We decided that Fiona and I would return to our house with the children and the fish in one car and leave the men to follow on, having cleared the nets completely and dismantled them, for they would not be used again until next August.

When we reached home the children galloped round the house in their usual high spirits. Fiona and I unloaded the fish and prepared some supper for the children, eventually chasing them up to bed even if they had little intention of going straight to sleep. There was always great excitement when other children came to stay, with chattering and laughter bubbling out of their bedrooms – girls in one room, the boys in another, even though they would creep into each other's room to tug away blankets or pillows, or maybe toys they thought someone else might want and just generally teasing each other until they became too tired to laugh and play any more and finally fell asleep.

Whilst the children were upstairs (I cannot say in their beds), Fiona and I started gutting the fish. Flounders are very easy to clean, a cut almost taking off the head followed by a quick pull and the job was done.

It was a blessing they were so easy to clean as we had an absolute mountain of fish to get through. We dropped the waste into a large bin and the fish (to be frozen and eaten) into a bucket filled with water to wash off sand and mud, and anything else that was sticking to them. There was a quick dip in another bucket of clean water before being drained and popped into bags ready for the deep freeze.

We had almost finished when the men arrived with another twenty pounds of fish, including a beautiful salmon bass which had not managed to leap over the net and had become entangled in the swirl of wire at the extreme end of the mesh curtain. Len and Fiona very generously insisted that we had the salmon as they had had plenty of them before; a meal we thoroughly enjoyed the following evening. It did not take Fiona and me long to finish cleaning the fish and dividing it between us whilst the men changed into some cleaner clothes and opened a bottle of wine; a drink well earned was the general opinion as we tucked hungrily into our supper.

Nothing was wasted from the fishing expedition; two families had enough fish to last them for six months and the pigs lived on the fish waste mixed with barley meal for a week. Not a bone was wasted. Pigs, we discovered through the years, will eat anything except grapefruit skins and tea leaves. Yes, a truly successful evening.

Chapter Thirteen

By September the outside of the house was practically complete. I had spent hours chipping away at the walls, the dust covering my face, filling my eyes and turning my hair into a king-size brillo pad. The first five feet were comparatively easy as this could be done standing on the ground or slightly elevated on an upturned milk crate, but the next five feet had to be tackled from the first stage of the scaffolding, which was reached by a short ladder. This too I managed. My problems started when I had to go even higher. I just do not like heights, and found once I had climbed the eighteen feet to the last stage I just froze on the last step of the ladder. I could not bring myself to step across the thirty-inch void, duck under the safety rail and onto the scaffolding boards which ran all round the house. Consequently, Malcolm would have to help me across the gap so that I could carry on doing the chipping out, and help me back again when either I was too tired to do any more or it was time to prepare a meal. That was fine at the weekends, but during the week it meant that I did not manage to clear so much stone as I could only work at it in the evenings when Malcolm was there to help me on and off the scaffolding.

It really was quite ridiculous – where was my will power? Non-existent by the look of things. So I decided that the next afternoon I would master that stupid gap. Leigh and Shelly were going to a birthday party straight after school and would not be brought home until six or seven o'clock. Malcolm would be home around five thirty, which only left me to contend with Bradley, and I knew that he would be quite happy to sit or stand in his play pen with all his favourite toys as long as he could see and talk to me even if I was in a somewhat elevated position. Plus of course the fact that he would be perfectly safe in his playpen if I did not manage to clamber back down the ladder – always supposing of course that I managed to get up the wretched thing.

I climbed the long, bouncing ladder and stood with my eyes closed tight until the wretched thing stabilised itself. I did not dare to look down. I stretched out one arm; I could just touch the scaffold support under the rail which I knew I would need in an endeavour to pull myself across the space from the ladder to the boards from which I would be working. I stood at the top of the ladder for about five minutes, the strain of which made my legs tremble. 'Come on,' I scolded myself, 'jolly well get on with it, you weak-willed wet' and suddenly, before I realised it, I was across the gap, hanging on to the scaffolding, shaking from head to toe – but at least I was across the gap and on the boards from which I would be working. Several deep breaths, then to attack the descent. That was easier because I could feel my way with my feet, and if they did not connect onto the right foothold at least I could hold onto the bars. I made it the first time. No one can appreciate the satisfaction gained from such a simple act unless they too are really scared of heights.

I spent about half an hour going up and down the ladder, crossing the gap and ducking under the rail. It was mastered. I did not tell Malcolm straight away what I had been doing but spent every minute I could chipping away at the stone. With more confidence now, in my elevated working position I seemed to work much quicker than when I was on the ground. After two days, I asked Malcolm to come and see how I was getting on with my labouring. He had been at the factory during the last two days and attending meetings for the last two evenings, not arriving home until dark, tired and ready for bed, so had not seen what I had been up to in his absence. He was amazed and delighted.

I was cross I had not mastered my fears sooner. The walls of the house were eventually rendered, then coated with a Tyrolean finish – a mixture of cement and colour wash which was mixed to a cream and put into a deep, narrow container from which protruded a handle. Prongs inside the container stuck out at right angles from a small drum connected to the handle which when turned covered the prongs with the creamy mixture and spat it against the wall – the thicker the mixture, the bigger the blob.

This finish seemed to be all the rage in the sixties; easy to apply and helpful in disguising any undulations that may occur in the rendering operation.

It took a little time to make the mixture of the same consistency each time, so we covered the back and sides of the house first so that by the time we reached the front we would have the finish one hundred per cent perfect. A complete transformation had taken place. We had formed a drive, put down concrete paths, built two walls at the entrance; Malcolm had even made a very decorative iron balustrade for the balcony he had constructed above the front door, and two iron scrolled chandeliers for the lounge.

We had really worked hard that summer and it was then that we were faced with a big decision. Malcolm's brother Dudley had gone to work in Kenya two years previously and was living with his wife and two children at Kabete, just outside Nairobi.

They had asked us many times to go out there for a holiday but previously it had been completely out of the question. Now we thought we should give the matter some serious consideration. First there were the children – Bradley was just two years old, could we leave him for a month or, more to the point, could I leave him? A couple of our very close friends were eager to have him and I knew he could not be left with anyone better, especially as he knew them so well, and they thought it was a wonderful opportunity for us that we should not miss.

We explained the situation to Leigh and Shelly and even at that tender age of six and a half and five and a half, they were anxious that we should enjoy a holiday in Africa. As they pointed out they would be having a holiday too with Giles and Emma (two other very close friends) and were quite happy to go to the local school with their children for the month. Again we knew they would be well looked after and probably spoilt to bits.

Malcolm then checked with Mr Finch that he would be able to take one month's holiday; the answer was yes, two weeks' allocation of holiday from one year adjoining two weeks from the next. We then needed confirmation that we were not likely to be moved – a possibility, as Malcolm had now been at the Carmarthen factory for seven years. 'Not a chance' was the reply from head office, not for another year at least. So that part was all right, particularly as we had a lot of internal work still to be done in the house.

Lastly, there were the pigs. 'We'll sell the lot,' said Malcolm. 'It's much too long a period to expect someone to come in and feed them.'

That seemed a bit drastic. 'Even the old sows?' I quavered.

'Yes. We'll start again when we get back; besides, it would probably be easier and more profitable to buy in slip at eight weeks than to start our own breeding again. We'll decide when we return in November.'

So that was it, the decision was made. The pigs were sold, plane tickets purchased, photographs, passports and all the other necessary arrangements made, culminating in the delivery of our children to our various friends.

I cried all the way home after leaving Bradley – my conscience was having its vengeance.

We left Heathrow on the 16th October, flying with Caledonian Airways on the noisiest of Comets, for the holiday of a lifetime. We had not had a proper holiday since our marriage in 1957 as we had always had livestock to be considered. Another reason for taking this opportunity with both hands was that Dudley and Iris might return to England the following year and the chance might be lost.

We spent just under three weeks in Kabete, and two weeks at Mombasa in a little bungalow amongst baobab trees and palms at Diani Beach. There were only two other dwellings there and they were over a hundred yards away. The locals were scraping seaweed from the rocks for food; a group of ten men, wearing only loose loincloths, squatted either side of a felled baobab trunk – hacking away the centre with their machetes and panga knives, turning it into a canoe right in front of our eyes. Colobus monkeys hung lazily along the branches of the huge baobab trees that grew close to the beach. An iguana, suddenly startled, ran across the volcanic rocks like a miniature, prehistoric dinosaur. The silent majesty of the elephants as they made their gentle way across the

Tsavo plain. Aloof giraffes, alert gazelles, zebra, wildebeest, hippos and rhino. We even found a huge deep cave almost big enough to house Wells Cathedral, used by thousands of fruit bats and the local witch doctor, complete with his strange little altar on which he apparently sacrificed chickens. The incredible sight of half a million flamingos wading on the shores of Lake Nakuru giving the water a delicate wash of rosy pink. Fishing for tilapia in Lake Naivasha, even catching some and cooking them on a barbeque.

The huge soda lakes at Magadi, an area so hot, bleak and barren that you are officially warned to take a guide and extra water. The colourful cockerel presented to Malcolm by one of Dudley's workers as a welcome present to Kenya; this was a very special gift as these people had very few possessions and any livestock was very coveted, so this was quite an honour for him. The time Malcolm and Dudley went shooting and left me in the car with a twelve bore, indicating with a wave of the hand that there was a rhino in the long grass about a quarter of a mile away, and were gone for two hours. There were some beautiful datura flowers growing on the side of a dried-out river bed some thirty yards from the car. I remember I had picked three of them when suddenly there was a terrific snort, a flurry of gazelles passed either side of me and I could clearly hear the crashing sounds of a large animal pushing through the undergrowth; the car horn was blowing and there were shouts from Malcolm and Dudley. I could not hear what they were shouting but I more than understood the urgency. I scrambled up the dusty bank and covered the open ground in no time at all. Dudley had the car engine running and we were off before my door was even closed

– a black rhino was left behind surrounded by a cloud of dust. I was then well and truly reprimanded for leaving the car, not a thing I would ever do again.

Yes, a truly fantastic holiday full of so many new experiences. We returned to London on the 21st November on the first public flight out of Nairobi on a VC10. There were just twenty-six passengers and six air hostesses. The press had had their flight yesterday but there was plenty of smoked salmon, caviar and champagne left for us, not forgetting the collection of top brand toiletries for both men and women in the very smart loos. A very different flight from the old lorry-like Comet that flew us out to Kenya.

The plane taxied right up to the observation balcony, the doors opened and we stepped out into the cold November air and were instantly greeted by screams and shouts from the platform above us. We looked up and there were Leigh and Shelly, together with Giles and Emma and their children, waving and shouting for all they were worth.

'Is that welcome for you?' asked one of the stewardesses. 'Goodness, I don't think the Beatles could have had a louder welcome.'

Giles and Emma had told the children they were going on a mystery tour; they had not dared to tell them that we might be on the plane in case of delays or any other problem that may have prevented our flight home. It was a really tremendous welcome back to England.

We collected Bradley from our other 'minder' friends, though they were not too keen on parting with him; they thought that perhaps he should stay the night and return home the next day. But we just all wanted to be together again – a complete family.

It did not take very long before we had settled down with our noses back to the grindstone. We had been back just nine days when Malcolm was summoned to Trowbridge.

We could not think why – perhaps they were objecting to the fact that we had stayed two days more than the allotted four weeks of holiday. Oh well, we would soon find out.

Malcolm came back very late that night. It was a long journey from Carmarthen to Trowbridge and back again, bearing in mind that the M4 had not yet been constructed. Even so, he did not look very tired and there was definitely an air of excitement about him. I could hardly wait to hear his news.

'You'll never guess,' said Malcolm following me into the lounge, 'so I may as well tell you straight away. We're being moved to Aylesbury; I'm to take over the factory from the present manager who is being moved to head office.'

'Aylesbury,' I gasped, 'but when?'

'Ah well, that's the um… er… problem. You see, darling,' he began, putting his arm round my shoulder. Alarm signals started to ring, but Malcolm went on talking. 'They want me to go to the Battersea factory on the first of January for a month, then on to Uttoxeter for three weeks, ending with a week at Torrington in Devon before taking over the Aylesbury factory as manager on the first of March.'

It was one of the rare occasions in my life that I was speechless. The full implications were gradually filtering through my befuddled mind. The house was nowhere near completion; decorating I could cope with, and I could probably do the roof insulation, but there was no way I could finish the central heating and of course we would have to find a buyer.

I looked at Malcolm and took a deep breath. 'Congratulations, my darling' and gave him a big hug. This was certainly a big step on the promotion ladder.

'I knew you'd be pleased. We'll lick this place into a saleable state in no time. Thank goodness we didn't start the pigs again, at least that's one thing we won't have to contend with, and we have over three weeks before I have to go up to London so I should easily finish the central heating by then. We may as well carry on and carpet the lounge as planned, it will make such a difference to the look of the whole place especially when you've finished the curtains (my first attempt with velvet), then with a bit of luck we'll be able to sell the lot with the house.'

Tears welled into my eyes. We had worked so hard on this, our first house, and would never have the pleasure of living in it. Then there were our friends (very special people), the first years of our married life, the birth of our children; already it was suddenly the past.

'I'll get some food on the go, you must be starving,' I mumbled, walking quickly to the safety and familiarity of the kitchen to give me time to pull myself and my thoughts together. My pioneering spirit was at a very low ebb.

Malcolm came into the kitchen five minutes later and sat down on one of the new stools. 'We're supposed to go to Aylesbury the day after tomorrow to look at the factory, look at the area and see what we think. If we really don't like what we see then we don't have to move, we can say no thank you and wait until something else turns up. We'll think it all through before we make a final decision.' Malcolm knew me better than I did.

We went to Aylesbury. There was no doubt as to what the decision would be. We were extremely lucky to be given this opportunity. It was an excellent time as far as the children's schooling was concerned and it would be lovely to live in England again and in such a lovely part of the country.

The next three weeks were soon gone; the central heating finished, the lounge wallpapered and the carpet laid on Christmas morning. We had a huge fire in the lounge on Christmas afternoon and had our presents from under the Christmas tree and spent the whole day with the children.

Malcolm left on New Year's Eve on the four o'clock train from Carmarthen. We made the mistake of taking the children to the station to see him leave. Leigh cried because he could not go on the train, Shelly cried because her daddy was going away and Bradley cried because he wanted his tea. I hoped that Malcolm did not see my tears as I tried to calm the children as the train pulled slowly away on its journey to London.

'I'll be back Friday evening,' Malcolm called and was gone. How empty the house was without him. It was no good moping. I stoked the fire in the lounge so that it would be lovely and warm in there after tea and cooked spaghetti Bolognese for the children – their favourite meal. Malcolm and I are not too keen on spaghetti so we did not have it very often. I fed the dogs and decided to let them stay in the house for the night; I suppose I was a little apprehensive about being on my own for the first time since we had been married.

I then read to the children for almost an hour from *The Wind in the Willows*, their favourite book, before tucking them into bed for the night.

January was a very long, cold month. Winston Churchill died – mourned by the nation – thousands passing solemnly by his coffin as he lay in state in Westminster Abbey.

I spent days sandpapering skirting boards, doors and window frames before I could paint them with undercoat, only to sandpaper them all again to a silk-like finish before covering the wood with glistening white gloss. At the end of the month we had a very heavy fall of snow and somehow during the ensuing blizzard one particular evening, the high winds brought down one of the heavy electricity cables that normally spanned two of the high-tension pylons nearby. Huge flickering sheets of blue light illuminated the whole of the area as bright as day. That night story time was by candlelight; luckily we had had tea and finished bath time before all power was lost. We were without electricity for two days. Unfortunately, it was bitterly cold, all the pipes in the roof and outside were frozen. I did not dare to light the fire in the lounge which normally would activate the radiators by the boiler that was set behind the fire, in case the water in the radiator pipes was frozen and somehow I might inadvertently cause an explosion. I spent hours melting snow and boiling it on top of the little camping gas ring before pouring it along the alkathene pipes in the uninsulated roof (insulation was the last job on our list unfortunately) catching the water in a bowl, reheating it on the gas ring before running it over the pipes again… I don't know why I bothered.

The house was so cold without the radiators being in use that we all slept together. At least we were warm, but little sleep was to be had.

I was so pleased to see Malcolm two days later; he had

had a terrible journey, cars and lorries abandoned all the way from Brecon to Carmarthen but the little Mini van – one of the first to have front wheel drive – came through with hardly a skid or problems of any sort.

We advertised the house in the *Journal* on the first Thursday in February, complete with planning permission for three houses in the paddock. A man came and looked at the house on Saturday and agreed to buy it straight away for the asking price. We just could not believe our luck. Completion day was set for the first of March, the very day Malcolm was due to take over the Aylesbury factory.

The days flew by, but we were able to finish the house completely to our satisfaction and pile clothes, toys and all our treasures into various boxes ready for removal day. Actually, we completed two days earlier than was at first expected, thus enabling us to see all our furniture and paraphernalia loaded onto the very large pantechnicon sent by one of the biggest removal companies in the country. Not a lowly tractor and trailer as this was an official company move; not that the contents of the company van varied that much to the old trailer.

Malcolm drove the old Thames van with children and dogs tightly bundled together; I drove the new Mini van complete with two hives full of bees. I'm not so sure that I really had the best deal. We arrived in Aylesbury at about eight o'clock that night feeling very tired, but we had to unload the bees first before we could turn our attention to the children or ourselves. We unloaded them at the back of the factory, the fronts of the hives facing across a large expanse of grass. I must say I was not at all sorry to part company with them; I was really worried the whole journey in case any bump should occur that would dislodge the small piece of wood placed at the front of the hives to keep the bees securely inside. We then drove to the Bell Hotel in the market square of Aylesbury where the company had booked rooms for us until such time as we found a house. We were made very welcome by the young couple who were managing the hotel at the time. The children were given a substantial hot supper before being tucked up or the night. They were all in one room which was obviously easier for the hotel and certainly the children were very happy with the arrangement. The dogs spent the night in the hotel garage before being taken to our friends Giles and Emma the next day. They had recently moved to a farm at Stratton Audley some fifteen miles away and had kindly said that they would have the dogs until we were settled in our own house.

Malcolm and I had a hot reviving shower and were ready for food ourselves. It was sheer bliss, someone else doing the cooking and clearing away, and joy to sink into a lovely comfortable bed. There had been no time today for sadness, a new era was about to start.

Chapter Fourteen

To find a house was our number one priority. It was obvious from the start that a smallholding would be completely out of the question, as ten-acre units just did not exist. Buckinghamshire, it seemed, was made up of very big farms or not quite such big farms; the only smallholdings were held by the local council. The houses came in similar sizes, very big, big, small and indifferent, but all considerably more expensive than anything one would find in West Wales. As the Easter holidays were about to start, we hoped that we would find a suitable house during this time so that the children could at least start school at the beginning of the summer term, even if we had not actually moved into a house but at least started the legal procedures into some sort of activity. We were looking for something within ten miles of Aylesbury so that Malcolm would not have too far to drive to the factory.

We soon discovered properties on the London side of Aylesbury were very much more expensive than anything to the north or west – that helped the search a little.

That first week I visited every house agent in Aylesbury and looked at or drove past every property that was on the market. The children were very good and seemed to enjoy this new game of 'house hunting'. They all had their own ideas as to the type of house we should buy, but they did agree on the need for a big garden. Shelly wanted a house with lots of loos of all things; Leigh wanted lots of trees. I don't think Bradley minded too much about anything as long as there was somewhere for him to sit down – he still was not the most energetic of children. (We obviously had no idea that in years to come he would more than make up for any idling now with his mountaineering achievements.) But a week was long enough to spend on house-hunting for the children; however, the second week only brought two properties to be inspected in the morning and so they would be taken swimming, for walks in the woods, to play in the park or cycling. We had visited a cycle dealer in Thame during our first weekend in Buckinghamshire and bought four second-hand bicycles. They were Leigh and Shelly's first two-wheelers, which they both mastered in the park behind the hotel.

Malcolm's bicycle looked like 'a country bobby bike', big, strong and black, accompanied by a deep clicking sound as the large wheels slowly turned. I drew the short straw. My bicycle did have a three speed attachment, but unlike Malcolm's three speed, it was not in working order; consequently I cycled everywhere in first gear. My bicycle also had the disadvantage of having had a small seat fitted behind the saddle, which unfortunately for me was just the right size for Bradley and for some obscure reason could not be fitted onto Malcolm's bicycle.

We had a lot of fun on the different jaunts we ventured on with the children, and it certainly helped to save our sanity during the many evenings and weekends that we were to spend at The Bell, and made a very pleasant change to Scrabble and Monopoly.

Four weeks passed, not a single house had appeared even as a slight possibility. I was beginning to get anxious, for the summer term was soon to start and we really did not want the children to miss any schooling, and it would have been very unsettling for them to start at one school only to find they would probably have to move to another once we had found a house.

One Saturday evening we visited our friends at Stratton Audley, Giles and Emma (the same couple who had looked after Leigh and Shelly whilst we were on our trip to Kenya). They told us about a house called The Villa in the nearby village of Steeple Claydon. From their description of the outside it sounded really lovely but the asking price was certainly far more than we had anticipated paying.

'We may as well go and have a look,' said Malcolm, 'at least we'll know what extras there are to be found with a more expensive house.'

'Why not give them a ring now? No time like the present,' urged Emma. 'After all, if they want to sell I should think they'd be only to pleased to see anyone. The name of the owners is Soleman.'

We soon found the number and waited impatiently for the telephone to be answered. It seemed an eternity before the ringing stopped, to be replaced by a very pleasant woman's voice, that of Mrs Soleman. Malcolm apologised for telephoning on a Saturday evening but explained that we had only just been told that their house was for sale and that we were very interested. There were no problems and it was arranged for us to go over to Steeple Claydon the next evening at seven o'clock.

Sunday could not pass quick enough for me. It would be fantastic if this house turned out to be the right one. Not too far from Aylesbury and Malcolm's factory, only four miles from our friends, and the children would be able to start school straight away at the school in the village – that was a real plus.

We found the house quite easily from our friends' description; apparently it was originally built as a hunting lodge in the late eighteen hundreds. We drove through the large double iron gates and up the short sloping drive, banked by half a dozen or so tall, lofty elm trees, which led us to the yellow front door of a larger-than-we-had-expected, Victorian, red-brick house. So far, so good. We were definitely impressed. We could see a well-kept spacious lawn running to the base of three leafy black poplars. Malcolm and I looked at each other both with the same question in our eyes – is this the very house for us?

'We'd better have a look inside,' Malcolm said calmly. 'You children must stay in the car for the time being; the Solemans won't appreciate all of us traipsing through their house.'

The children protested but did as they were told, their noses pressed flat to the car windows in an endeavour to see as much as possible. The door opened before we had a chance to use the heavy shining brass knocker, not that it was really necessary anyway, the deep baying of some very large dog within the house was enough to announce our arrival to the whole village. Mrs Soleman opened the door, immediately inviting us inside but not before she had seen the children in the car.

'Oh, you must bring the children in,' she insisted, 'it doesn't seem right to leave them outside; they can play with our four whilst I show you round the house.'

Needless to say, the children did not need to be asked twice. They leapt out of the car as quick as a star's twinkle; even Bradley seemed to be motivated for once, scrambling after the others as fast as his little legs could carry him. They disappeared into the garden, leaving us standing in the spacious, red-carpeted entrance hall. We walked from one light airy room to another. The views from the dining room and kitchen were quite magnificent – thirty miles of fields and woodland, right across the Vale of Aylesbury. This lovely warm Victorian house with two acres of garden and a pond was just what we wanted, but could we afford the asking price?

Mrs Soleman interrupted my thoughts by saying, 'We've seen everything here, so we'll go and have a look at the stable cottage. We only had the conversion done last year but it really is very quaint.'

The owner led us out through the front door and started walking on round the drive, which turned out to be circular, something we had not noticed in our excitement when we first came up the drive. Again Malcolm and I exchanged glances as Mrs Soleman guided us over a little cobbled forecourt, through the front door and into the tiny hall of the little cottage. Three doors confronted us, revealing a kitchen, a bathroom and a surprisingly spacious lounge with dark timbers which reached high into the roof. We then turned and mounted a wrought-iron spiral staircase to the single bedroom which was above the kitchen and bathroom – again with a timbered ceiling; the whole interior looked Tudor in style and very cosy.

'How on earth did you manage to carry the bed and that huge wardrobe upstairs?' I asked as we clattered back down the spiral staircase.

'Oh, the removal men put ropes round everything, then hauled each piece of furniture up the outside wall and swung each item through the bedroom window. It was much easier than you would expect.'

Immediately adjoining the cottage was a large double

garage; across the ceiling a wire mesh sheet had been suspended and used for apple storage. Some of last season's Bramleys still remained – all picked from the garden. I had always wanted to have apple trees, something to do with my towny upbringing, I suppose.

'Well, that's everything apart from the vegetable garden at the back of the house; we'll walk back that way and see what the children are up to and perhaps you'd like a cup of coffee.'

We walked slowly back to the house and passed the good-sized vegetable patch and apple trees. Malcolm and I looked at each other and we both nodded in unison; this was definitely the house we would like to buy. We checked that the children were behaving themselves and joined the Solemans for a cup of coffee in the kitchen.

We clarified the asking price for the property but found to our consternation that the Solemans had already been offered the full amount by someone else through the estate agents, but as yet nothing had been signed or any contact made by agents or solicitors, and that was three weeks ago. We, on the other hand, had discovered the property privately, so no agents were involved from our side.

'What if we were to offer you your asking price?' said Malcolm. 'It would mean that you would receive the full amount as there wouldn't be any agents' fees to pay. We don't have a house to sell, the money is available and we're ready to move in without delay, subject of course to a satisfactory survey.'

I held my breath, wondering what the Solemans would say; wondering how we would raise the extra money involved.

The Solemans looked at each other then at us.

'I don't see why not,' said Mr Soleman. 'It would certainly suit us; all the legalities have been sorted out on the house that we are buying, it's only a question of our final signature. As far as your survey is concerned, you can have a look at the roof and drains etc whenever you like; you can also have a look at the survey report carried out by a local firm for someone else who was interested but was unable to go ahead with the purchase due to some personal reasons.'

We eventually left the Solemans, armed with a complete survey of The Villa, parting with a firm handshake, having settled the deal verbally and confirming that we would contact solicitors in the morning to do the necessary paperwork.

Having rounded up the children and hustled them into the car, we tried to hush their excited questions, at least until we had driven out of earshot.

'Are we going to buy it?'

'Can we live there?'

'Can I have the bedroom with the pink curtains?'

'Can I climb the tallest tree?'

'Did you know there were four toilets?'

The children were so excited, as we were ourselves. We endeavoured to explain to the children that there were a few things to be sorted out first, but we would buy the house if we could and we would know for sure in a few days' time. Not a very satisfactory answer as far as they were concerned but it was the best we could manage.

Once the children were in bed, we were able to talk things through properly.

'Can we really afford to pay such a high price?' I asked.

'Well,' said Malcolm, 'I know it's more than we expected to pay, but we'll have more than we expected to buy. I realise we shall be down to practically a nil balance, in fact, we may have to take up some money from the bank – but that's better than having a mortgage.' (I suppose we were both a little old fashioned; for some reason we both hated the idea of a mortgage or borrowing money and wanted to be able to pay for our house, or anything we owned, without owing money to anyone. However, on this occasion we may have to bend our ideal a little.) 'We'll see what the survey shows, but I still want to have a look for myself.'

At least after renovating Waunffordd, we had a very good idea of what to look for and how to cure any problems should there be any waiting for us. It transpired that the worse problem was (to quote from the professional survey) 'evidence of some woodworm infestation is apparent in four roof timbers on the west side of the house.' This was not much of a problem at all. Malcolm carried out his own survey and confirmed the woodworm problem, but it was only superficial. The timbers were as hard as iron, all that was needed was a good spraying of woodworm killer. Malcolm was more concerned about the joists under the floor boards; these apparently needed attention, with replacement being necessary for some of the timbers. Again though, nothing that we could not do ourselves.

It was a lovely house, I could hardly believe that we had been so lucky.

Completion day was set for four weeks' time, during which period I was easily able to ferry the children backwards and forwards to the village school, always driving past The Villa just to have a gloating look. The

Villa – what a funny old-fashioned name it was. Built with red brick as a hunting lodge in 1888 on land purchased for the amazing sum of £385. Stables had been built at the entrance gates and there was a paddock where the horses could stay and rest between hunts. A pond had been dug out of the heavy clay so that they had access to water. The pond was still there, surrounded by elegant ash trees and swaying willows. The paddock had been sold off and a house built on it in the 1930s. We decided that we would change the name of the house from The Villa to Hunters Lodge – its original purpose in life, built so that the owners and their friends had somewhere very comfortable to stay when they came to visit and, of course, hunt.

Time passed fairly quickly before yet another moving day dawned. Leigh and Shelly were deposited at the school gates as usual, after which I drove back up the hill to the house to await the arrival of the removal van and however many men they had sent to unload all our worldly possessions. They arrived at nine thirty. Carpets, furniture and boxes were pulled out of the large van and trundled in through the front door before being placed, or dumped in, hopefully the right rooms. I must say the men were very good and helped me to put down the bedroom carpets so that at least the beds could be put in their proper places. The lounge and dining-room furniture was stacked against the walls in those two rooms as we had decided we would attend to the repair work to the floor joists before buying a new carpet; it would also be an added incentive to get the job done as quickly as possible.

Eventually the van was empty and the men left, leaving Bradley and myself to turn our new nest into something resembling a home. We would have a few hours to ourselves before Leigh and Shelly came home from school and Malcolm returned from the factory, where he had been holding meetings all day. Boxes were emptied, cupboards filled, clothes put on hangers, china stacked into the kitchen units, packets and tins vying for space on the numerous shelves. It was while I was making up the beds that I first heard the sound of running water. I ran from one bedroom to another, then quickly downstairs, checking each room; no sign of water anywhere. I squinted at the stopcock under the kitchen sink and turned it off as an added precaution. I went back upstairs and back into the front bedroom where I had been making our bed. I pulled the eiderdown straight then heard the running water again. I ran out onto the landing; nothing. It really was most odd. I had visions of floods of water in one of the rooms, but which one. Perhaps a pipe had burst in the roof and the water had not reached the bedrooms yet. I went straight back into our bedroom and stood still. Nothing. Then, softly at first the sound of bubbling water, more like a mountain stream than tap water. I ran to the window and there in front of my eyes, was the cause. The three huge Italian black poplars were swaying in the gusting breeze, the leaves rustling against each other as they twirled by their long slender stems, like paddles in the wind. I was so relieved. It was quite an experience and incredible to believe that leaves could really sound like running water. We have through the years planted many poplars, as much for the sound of their leaves as their majestic beauty.

The move into our new home was completed fairly painlessly and we settled down to a fairly normal family life. Over the next eighteen months, Malcolm organised the factory to his satisfaction; we put the house and garden in order and started a badminton club in the village hall. Bradley started school.

Shelly joined the Brownies and Leigh joined the Cubs. On the first visit to the Cubs meeting place – a village hall in the next village – I was pounced on by Akela, leader of the pack, and invited to help each week for just an hour with the dear little Cubs. I recognised many of the nice little faces from my daily trip to the school gates and I must say those little boys looked really smart in their cub uniform. I thought it would be a good idea to become involved, after all it would only be for an hour or maybe two hours each week and it was certainly a worthwhile organisation as far as the youngsters were concerned.

I told Akela that I would be delighted to help. I was a little taken aback with her enthusiasm at my offer, but thought no more about it at the time. However, within five minutes of stepping into the village hall the nice little boys whom I had recognised from my daily trips to the school gates had turned into howling, leaping demons who could scramble onto the top of a cupboard, throw themselves into space shouting 'Geronimo' at the top of their voices, land on your back and bring you to the ground in four seconds flat.

After five encounters with the very hard floor, I avoided all high-rise cupboards. I'm afraid I only lasted as Akela's assistant for four weeks but tentatively offered my services to the Wise Owl who ran the Brownies. This was a much quieter affair and very satisfying but unfortunately due to lack of numbers, the little group of Brownies was disbanded. So I indulged myself and joined the local tennis club instead. We still had the bees of course, with all the work they seemed to generate, though this was somewhat sporadic.

I then started going to art classes at the Aylesbury Technical College. Although for only one day a week it was stimulating and I learnt a great deal about painting, though I feel it is something I will never really master but always enjoy. Malcolm became a founder member of the Aylesbury Junior Chamber of Commerce and also decided to take up rugby again after a break of ten years.

This involved the whole family, as all the children played together and watched a little rugby; the wives all talked together and also watched a little rugby before preparing the teas serving them to the players. Always a most enjoyable afternoon, especially if we won. The rugby club social events were always good fun and a great success, especially the fancy dress nights when everyone made an effort.

One would think this quite a satisfactory way of life, but one evening after supper, Malcolm suggested that perhaps we should do something more constructive with our spare time. I was not too sure what spare time he was talking about, but I am always prepared to listen.

'What do you think about the idea of building a house on the land to the side of the pond?'

I looked at Malcolm in utter amazement. 'Build a house,' I stammered. 'But we're not proper builders.' Malcolm was not to be deterred.

'Building a house is just a series of jobs and a builder is someone who reckons that he can do all of them and I'm pretty certain we could do most of them and… if we do get stuck then we'll call in the experts. Waunffordd was no problem at all, we pretty well covered most building aspects there and building from scratch should be much easier than converting an existing building.

'Besides, the council always inspect every house under construction at different stages so they'd very soon tell us if anything was wrong. What do we have to lose? Absolutely nothing. What do we have to gain? Lots. Building experience, doing something for ourselves, and hopefully a house to sell at the end to help swell the family coffer.'

What could I say? It seemed such a big project and yet I knew what Malcolm said was true. It really was something that we could do and something that we would enjoy doing. I was slowly beginning to feel some enthusiasm. 'How long do you think it would take?' I asked my budding Christopher Wren.

'Difficult to say, but I would have thought about two years if we do it all ourselves. Though I do feel that we shouldn't put ourselves under any time pressure or it will become a chore and not something to enjoy.'

'What about planning permission?' I queried.

'I shouldn't think that would be too much of a problem as it would be classed as in-filling and councils I believe, are normally quite happy about that type of development.'

'What type of house should we build, and what about the plans?' I was full of questions.

'I've been thinking about that myself. I believe there's a book that has been published with many different designs of houses together with detailed plans, though I think a bungalow would probably be the easiest especially as it's our first venture.'

'I'll ask in the library tomorrow,' I said, 'they're sure to know.'

'Let's take a cup of coffee and inspect our possible

building plot and see if we can assess exactly what would be involved.'

We wandered over to the far side of the garden and looked at the area in question. Up until now we had just cut the grass up to the side of the pond to keep it tidy, but because of its shape it never really seemed to be a part of the garden so its loss would not really detract from our property.

'An overlap fence would probably be the answer,' said Malcolm. 'It would soon blend in and we could grow some shrubs against it as added camouflage. Of course, the first job would be to cut down the trees around the pond.' We looked at the four forty-feet high, billowing willows and the two sixty-feet spreading ash trees. It did seem a pity to cut them down but their shadows were creeping ever closer to the house and kept a considerable amount of light from the lawn and flower beds, and it would not be long before they became a danger to the property itself. The trees would certainly have to go, if we decided to build or not.

'We would then have to fill in the pond,' Malcolm said thoughtfully. When we first moved into the village we had tried to determine the depth of the pond and discovered that beneath the top six inches of very dark water lay five feet of thick, slimy, rotten vegetation that had probably deepened each autumn since the turn of the century.

'Goodness knows how many lorry-loads of hard core would be needed – plus fine and coarse scalpings, finished with about eighteen inches of topsoil. The filled-in pond area would make a lovely lawn, and there would be plenty of space for the house to be built well clear of the old pond area. I could imagine that one would encounter all sorts of problems trying to build on made up land – one would have to build a raft or something, but luckily we don't have that problem.'

'How much space do you think the house would require?' I asked. It's one thing to walk into a house and decide whether you like it or not, but to contemplate how much space is needed to actually build a house is a completely different matter.

'We shall have to see what type of design is the most practical and of course suitable for that area, but I would have thought if we allowed about forty feet from the front door to the back door plus a small garden at the front we would have ample room,' replied Malcolm.

There was no doubt in either of our minds that this project could be very satisfying, and certainly quite exciting and something that we could do whenever we felt like it, unlike the animals that we had kept in the past, which had forced us into a regular routine and gave problems as far as holidays and weekends away were concerned. With the decision made to get started on our exciting project, I could hardly wait for morning to come so that I could invade the local library to find out what they knew about any books that might have house plans and designs.

Chapter Fifteen

The library opened at ten o'clock – needless to say I was their first customer. I told the lady at the desk what I was looking for and asked her if she had any ideas as to the titles of any such book. She surpassed all expectations. With great delight she told me that probably the book that I was looking for was called *Plan Your Home* and was available at any reputable bookshop for the princely sum of two pounds, but it so happened that if I wanted to borrow a copy from the library – and this year's edition was available – in fact she had a copy on the shelf.

I couldn't have been more delighted and the librarian was very pleased with herself into the bargain. I hurried home clutching the book that I hoped would contain the details of our future building project. I decided not to look at the book until Malcolm and I could sit down and study it together.

As soon as Malcolm came in that evening I could not help teasing him by saying, 'You'll never guess what I've got.'

His answer was, 'You'll never guess what I've got.'

We produced our 'surprises'. Malcolm was amazed that I had actually managed to get hold of the book of plans and I was more than surprised when he waved a wad of papers under my nose, saying with great delight 'Planning application forms in triplicate and the information that planning permission normally only takes about four weeks from receipt of plans to actual decision.'

We spent the evening poring over the many designs – anything from six bedrooms, three-bathroomed mansions with balconies and terraces to one bedroom, lounge/diner bungalows.

Although at first we thought we could only manage a bungalow, we eventually decided that as one must put a roof on a bungalow we may as well make a slightly bigger roof and use the roof space for bedrooms. We finally decided on a design called Avon – it looked like a bungalow from the front but the back had a large dormer built into the long sloping roof which gave space for two bedrooms and a bathroom plus loads of sloping roof space for storage purposes. The downstairs plan showed a lounge twenty-eight feet by fifteen feet, a dining room, one other bedroom and a kitchen, a fairly basic design and one that we felt we could manage.

Things were certainly beginning to move. All through our married life once we had made a decision to do something we could not wait to start the project and finish as soon as possible.

I remember many years later an elderly neighbour of ours in Somerset saying, 'You never know what they Bakers are going to do until they've done it.' We took this as a great compliment.

Preparing plans for the council would be the next job. Malcolm decided that he would like to attempt these himself – after all, it was basically only a matter of copying and enlarging the plans printed in the *Plan Your Home* book, which clearly listed the correct materials to be used and correct construction procedure – stress and strains for timbers, etc, all worked out by the qualified architect of Avon. Our job was to carry out his instructions. We would also have the safety net of regular inspections by the council to make sure everything was in accordance with building regulations. And, if necessary we could always call on a professional builder.

Malcolm spent the next six evenings copying out the plans. Three original sets had to be submitted to the local council, together with all the relevant forms. By the time they were completed, I must say that they looked quite professional and as Malcolm said, even if the plans were not accepted, he had enjoyed drawing them up and had learned quite a lot in the process. We took some Photostat copies for ourselves before handing them in to the planning department in Aylesbury. We knew that we would have to wait about a month for the big decision.

I have never known time to pass so slowly; although we wanted to build the house, we did not want to cut down the trees or fill in the pond until we knew for certain that we had planning permission because we both felt that if planning was refused we would clean up the pond area and make it into a more interesting feature and extension to our garden.

However, we were in luck. Planning permission was granted. With the letter came a little bundle of inspection cards, which had to be filled in and sent to the council each time certain parts of the house construction were completed so that they could be examined and passed as sound according to the building regulations. So, to the first job – the removal of the trees. We could not saw the trees down close to the ground as this would have caused too much damage as they crashed onto our garden. So each tree had to be dismembered branch by branch.

It was late autumn. All the trees had shed their leaves so at least we could see quite clearly each and every branch that had to be removed. It seems incredible now, but all we had to carry out this mammoth task was a thirty-one inch, basic bow saw and a billhook.

The plan was that Malcolm would cut off the branches as close to the trunk as possible and my job was to trim off all the side shoots, putting them to one side to be burnt later on a bonfire. I would then have the privilege of hauling the larger pieces over to the shed near the house ready to be sawn into logs for the house fires.

All went well – we trimmed the branches from all the trees up to a height of about fifteen feet. After that height Malcolm said that he wanted me to stand on the bottom rung of the ladder to give it more rigidity as he sawed away at the higher branches.

'Now, don't forget, whatever happens, don't move off that bottom rung until I am back down, safely on the ground,' came the instructions from my beloved husband-turned-lumberjack.

I stood firmly on the bottom rung and looked up to see how Malcolm was progressing with a particularly large branch, only to be rewarded with clouds of gritty sawdust filling my eyes. I tried squinting, my head craned right back, but this only gave me a crick in the neck. So I decided just to stand still and look at the garden around me, thinking my own thoughts and trying to decide what we should have for dinner that evening. I then heard a large, muffled plop and was immediately covered with a mantle of black, evil-smelling sludge from the pond, as the branch that Malcolm was sawing fell into its murky depths.

'Oh, sorry darling, did you uh… get splashed?' asked my beloved gaily from above.

'Splashed,' I complained bitterly. 'I'm soaked to the skin, I stink like a pole cat and I'm cold, tired and hungry.' I think Malcolm came to the conclusion that I was not very happy with my present position in life.

'What if we just cut off these last couple of branches and then call it a day? We've done pretty well really.'

I was somewhat appeased; the thought of a nice hot cup of tea and a hot shower was certainly heartening.

'You're still standing on the ladder I hope?' Malcolm queried.

'Yes, of course I am – I wouldn't want to be doing anything else,' I fibbed.

The sawing continued – one more branch fell into the pond. I became even wetter. I said not a word, but many words went through my mind. 'Last one now' – more sawing. Sawdust covered my head and shoulders like a massive cloak of dandruff. There was an ominous tearing sound as the half-sawn branch above tore its shattered limb away from the main trunk and fell to earth. I suddenly felt a hot, searing pain in my right shoulder; the sawn end of the falling branch had struck me a hefty glancing blow just before embedding itself in the grassy turf at the foot of the ladder. It felt as if my arm had been severed from my body. It was completely numb. I just could not move. I remained standing on the ladder, thoroughly dazed.

'Are you all right?' Malcolm shouted as he clambered quickly down the ladder, mumbling something about the end of the sawn branch catching in the adjacent tree and twisting as it fell.

I was not at all interested in any reasons why, or the cause in the change of intended direction of that wretched branch. As soon as Malcolm was four rungs above my head, I stepped off the ladder and made purposefully for the house.

My arm hung limply at my side. Tears coursed down my face but no noise came; I did not seem to be able to cry or speak. I suppose it was shock. Malcolm ran after me and attempted to put his arm around my shoulder. I shrugged him off. I was in no mood to be forgiving. I hated those trees and I certainly was not going to stand on that wretched ladder again.

Malcolm did not speak – he walked quietly with me to the house and into the kitchen and guided me into a chair. I sat stiffly, looking at him through my silent tears. Then I began to laugh and cry at the same time.

A big smile replaced the worried concern on Malcolm's face. 'Thank goodness for that – I really thought things were serious.'

'They are serious,' I howled. 'I don't think my right arm will ever be the same again'. Already the throbbing had started.

'Let's get that anorak off and have a look,' Malcolm said more seriously. He gently eased my unbending arm out of the jacket and slowly drew my jumper over my head and down the aching limb. The skin was not broken but an angry, red, swollen lump with blue undertones, the size of a fifty pence piece, straddled my shoulder, right on the joint. With some apprehension I allowed Malcolm to move my arm backwards and forwards but objected strongly to it being lifted. He gently probed the swollen area with his fingers.

'Um…' A slight pause. 'I don't think anything is broken; your jacket and sweater probably saved you. In fact, I don't know what all the fuss is about. He leapt nimbly to one side as I lashed out with my feet.

'Well it jolly well feels like it,' I complained.

Needless to say, nothing was broken and after a few

days' partial rest all was well and back to normal. We spent the next couple of weekends de-limbing the trees; the ladder, when in use, being weighted or strapped to the trunk of the relative tree whilst I stood well clear. We were now left with only the crowns. They looked like huge nests, swaying drunkenly from lofty masts in a strong wind.

Malcolm made a cut about four feet below the highest small branch that we could not quite reach with the ladder, and started sawing through the stark white wood. The brittle timber cracked open when he was just two thirds across the trunk. The crown toppled and swung lifeless against the supporting stump, held only by a thin strip of bark. Gradually the swaying sticks (for that was all they were – their days of glory finished) tore themselves slowly from the tree's protection and fell to the ground to be joined later by the remainder of the trunk, which was cut into neat four-feet logs except for the jagged teeth that persisted in emerging with each sawn length, as if in protest.

Eventually, we were left with just ten feet of trunk, and roots which still lay solidly beneath the damp November soil.

'We'll stack all the logs against the far fence, that will give us some space to deal with the roots.'

'Exactly how are you going to get rid of the roots?' I queried.

'Well, you know that I managed to borrow a winch; I'm hoping that we'll be able to prise the roots out of the ground.'

I watched with great interest as Malcolm placed a steel cable around the trunk of the smallest tree. Some nine feet from the ground, the diameter of the tree was about eighteen inches. He secured it with a slip knot then ran the cable through the winch, which was anchored to another tree. Malcolm then pulled the handle, which was on a ratchet, backwards and forwards. The loose cable was taken through the winch and gradually it tightened until all the strain was on the winch. With very little effort the tree started to lean over slowly and sedately. As it was lowered gently to rest by the side of the pond, the roots left the soft soil with very little protest. So far so good. But not all the trees were prepared to give in so gracefully. Some were decidedly obstinate. This was basically due to the fact that as more roots were removed the strategic position of the winch became more and more difficult to find – resulting in backbreaking spade-work and yet more sawing. We had cut all the trees down except for the last two, and as I needed to pop into Buckingham for some groceries I left Malcolm to start on the trees, promising to be back in about an hour. Which I was, loaded like the proverbial pack horse. I could see that he was still fighting the good fight and shouted to him that some coffee would be ready in about ten minutes.

I was still unpacking the shopping when Malcolm suddenly staggered into the kitchen the side of his head and face covered in blood and more blood oozing through his fingers as they searched to staunch the flow from the side of his head. I was horrified.

'What on earth have you done?' I gasped. I quickly guided him on to a chair and gently moved his hands to inspect the wound.

His ear was split from the top down for about two inches, but luckily there was no actual head wound. 'It was the winch,' he groaned. 'I had the strain on maximum, wrestling with one of those wretched roots. I knew that I would have to pull from another direction before the roots would give; unfortunately, when I released the tension, the handle was up and not down as it should have been and it whipped over and hit me on the side of the head and knocked me clean off my feet.'

A long ugly bruise was appearing just behind the temple. I dread to think what would have happened if the lever had struck Malcolm just two inches further forward. I swabbed Malcolm's split ear with a very strong solution of salty water but still the blood continued to flow.

More pressure was needed to try and staunch the bleeding. We decided the best way was for Malcolm to hold a sodden wad of cotton wool against the ear. I glanced at Malcolm's face, covered in mud and blood. He looked so dejected and sorry for himself, I just could not help laughing.

'I can't see what's so funny,' he grumbled.

'You would if you could see yourself. You look like an old tom cat that's been in an alley fight and lost. Your ear is hanging down in two pieces. Even so, I think you'll have to go into hospital and have it stitched.'

Although I did not say anything, I was concerned that we could not stop the bleeding, and it could be that Malcolm was also slightly concussed, especially as he did not protest at all when I suggested that we leave straight away for the hospital in Aylesbury. After the twenty-minute drive, the towelling pad which Malcolm had been holding to his head was completely sodden with blood. In fact it was trickling down his hand and up his sleeve. He looked in a real pickle. We went straight into the casualty department – it was obviously a quiet day for there were no other casualties to be seen. I walked up to the desk and asked the fairly elderly nurse enthroned there if my husband could please see a doctor as soon as possible as he had had an accident and cut his ear very badly.

'I should think so,' she said, showing very little interest. 'Tell him to sit over there,' and waved her hand at the six rows of empty chairs.

We sat, Malcolm with his bloody head resting on his bloody hands as more blood dripped onto the clean hospital floor. We sat in silence for four minutes before I exploded. My concern for Malcolm was just too much, the pain so obvious in his eyes. I marched up to the desk and asked the matriarch sitting there when were we likely to receive some attention.

'My husband has received a hefty blow on the side of his head, he has practically split his ear in two and he's bleeding all over your clean floor.'

The last six words obviously had some impact, but we still did not receive the attention that was required.

'Blood on the floor!' she gasped. 'What's his name, date of birth and religion?'

'What has that got to do with it?' I hissed between clenched teeth, my patience at a very low ebb. 'My husband needs some medical attention immediately – can you please find someone to attend to him now? I can give you all the information that you want whilst he's being treated.'

The matriarch looked at me, looked at Malcolm and then looked at her floor. I think it occurred to her that the longer she delayed, the longer the blood would be on her floor.

Once she had made the decision to move, within two

minutes we found ourselves being very quickly ushered into the treatment room. A little dark-skinned doctor appeared through the door like a genie from a lamp.

'Oh now, what is the trouble,' he said, bobbing up and down on his very short legs. 'Let me see.' He very gently eased the sodden, bloody mass of cotton wool away from the side of Malcolm's head.

'Oh my goodness me!' he exclaimed. 'It is broken through and through.' And promptly plonked the bloody dressing back over Malcolm's ear.

It did not look as if he liked the sight of blood either. 'Can't touch,' he declared. 'You must go to plastic surgery at Stoke Mandeville,' and practically pushed us out of the door. Back into the Mini and a fairly nippy drive across Aylesbury took us to Stoke Mandeville hospital some ten minutes later. It then took another ten minutes to find the right department. Thankfully by this time the bleeding had eased, though Malcolm's hands did not look very healthy to the untrained eye. At Stoke Mandeville the treatment was completely different. As soon as we walked into the plastic surgery unit a nurse immediately took Malcolm away to the treatment room; she asked me if I would like a cup of tea before asking for any details.

We must have looked quite a sorry pair. Malcolm looked very grey and was I suppose still in a state of shock. I felt grey and very shattered, but ten minutes of peace and quiet and the tea made me feel much more human, and when Malcolm appeared an hour later with a clean face, some colour in his cheeks and, miraculously, a whole ear, I felt almost normal. Poor Malcolm, though back in one piece, had a lousy headache which took a few days to clear. But at least he still had a pair of ears.

It was Boxing Day. We had had a succession of severe frosts which had left the pond with a glistening cloak of ice some two inches thick. Malcolm said that he would like to saw off the three remaining branches on the last tree to be de-limbed and then afterwards perhaps we could take the children to Buckingham to see the meet of the local hunt in the Market Square; always a colourful affair and a new experience for the children.

Malcolm pulled on his Wellingtons and departed for the pond area armed with his chainsaw. The children stayed in the house with me and played with each other's Christmas presents. It was safer to have the youngsters inside than on the loose outside whilst we were operating on the trees.

I had just finished putting the finishing touches to some sausage rolls when I heard a clatter and banging at the back door. I opened the door, thinking that it was one of the dogs jumping against the door for attention or perhaps a bone – but no. I gasped in shock and amazement at the sight that met my eyes. Malcolm was leaning against the wall, covered in black, stinking slime, shaking uncontrollably and unable to speak coherently. What on earth had happened? But this was no time to wait for any garbled, unintelligible reply. Somehow he had fallen into the frozen pond and was badly shaken.

I quickly pulled off all Malcolm's clothes and, with great difficulty, his Wellingtons, which seemed to be fixed to his feet with very strong suction pads. I then helped him up the stairs to the bathroom where I ran a fairly cool bath. He managed (with some assistance) to lower himself into the bath, to which I gradually added more hot water as his body was able to take a higher temperature. After about fifteen minutes he took on the healthy glow of a well-cooked lobster and managed a wry smile and was able to tell me exactly what had happened.

He had in fact sawn off the top branch of the last tree by standing on the branch below it and reaching up above shoulder level. No problems. The top branch, which overhung the pond bank, dropped to the ground as planned. Malcolm had then climbed onto the bottom branch and again reached up with the bow saw and had sawn three quarters of the way through the middle branch. When it tore itself away from the tree, it twisted and hit the branch on which he was standing. This left him with nothing to hold to help him keep his balance. He knew if he jumped he would not be able to reach the bank; the only way down was, into the pond. So into the pond he went, feet first. He thought that he would reach the bank fairly easily, but the ice on the pond just broke into huge sheets which reared up in front of him as he threw his weight forward onto them. He then found himself slipping back into the water.

He had tried several times without success, all the time becoming colder and colder. He then noticed that a couple of the ice sheets had piled one on top of the other and this was just strong enough to take his weight and enabled him to grasp some of the branches that lay on the side of the pond and was gradually able to pull himself to safety.

It had taken several minutes before he had managed to reach the house but he was not able to open the door; he could only lean against the door and knock feebly, and he was not exactly welcomed with open arms when the door was opened.

We've laughed many times through the years that Malcolm was not let into the house until he was stripped of all his clothes, but the incident could have ended quite differently.

Meanwhile the children, not really able to appreciate the situation, were wondering why and how Malcolm had come to fall in the dirty old pond when we were supposed to be getting ready to take them to see the local hunt meet in Buckingham. I looked at Malcolm and asked the question.

'Do you really feel like going out when you should really stay at home in the warm?'

'Can't disappoint them, can we?' He smiled.

So… we ate the sausage rolls that had been very well heated for about three quarters of an hour, devoured a quick bowl of soup and set off for Buckingham. There must have been about two hundred spectators, at least eighty horses and their riders and of course a large pack of hounds. One gentleman in particular was quite outstanding – a big, heavy, elderly man wearing a puce jacket that matched the colour of his face, astride a magnificent chestnut gelding. He looked as if he was a century late for this Boxing Day meet – Jane Eyre would not have looked out of place at his side. Many ladies riding side-saddle wore long flowing skirts and smart pillbox hats with hair tucked up inside or heavy hair nets holding their shiny locks high off square, set shoulders. There were smartly dressed kennel lads who served little glasses of steaming punch from silver trays to all the hunt riders and followers. The whole scene was a perfect Christmas card, a lovely way to end the Christmas celebrations, and the children experienced an event to remember for years to come.

Now that all the trees were down, logged and stacked, our next job was to fill in the pond. We were lucky enough to hear about some obsolete buildings that were being pulled down at a factory in Aylesbury.

So… twenty ten-ton loads of broken bricks, concrete and asphalt were dumped in the murky pond, covered with a couple of lorry-loads of topsoil – with the result that we had a garden adjoining our building plot.

With planning permission given for us to build the three-bedroom house called Avon that we had chosen from the book *Plan Your Home*, we were ready to start. Foundations first. No mini digger or JCB for us, just a pickaxe, spade, wheelbarrow and muscle. We plotted the outline of the house with string, followed by an inner string to mark the width of the foundations for the four outside walls and dug trenches two feet six inches deep and two feet wide – these being the main load-bearing walls.

We then dug smaller ditches eighteen inches deep and eighteen inches wide for the low load-bearing walls on which the room partitions would be built. This took four enthusiastic evenings and a full slower Saturday to complete.

'So how are you going to get the levels right?' I enquired – knowing that we did not own or have access to a Cowley level (every surveyor's secret weapon).

'No problem,' came the reply. 'We'll use the hosepipe and water level method to get the levels right, plus another six inches to over site level. Simple.'

'Is that how they built the pyramids?' I was beginning to get the measure of my husband after eight years of marriage, but my comment was totally ignored.

Actually, it worked. A hosepipe was placed along the length of each foundation trench – a glass tube at one end, a funnel at the other; water was poured down the funnel into the hosepipe and this flowed along the pipe until it reached the glass tube at each end of the trench. The water settled, found its level and the wooden stakes that had been pushed into the trench, next to the glass tubes, were duly marked. The levels were then checked all the way along each trench – hey presto, everything in 'level' order.

I was told with great authority that the footing trench must be deep enough to ensure that when the concrete blocks were cemented in place, the top block must be six inches above ground level; and we did not forget to put in the mains water pipe. The following weekend we had a delivery of high density concrete blocks and a load of ready-mix cement and were able to level the whole site and set out the different rooms one block high, leaving the appropriate gaps for doorways. I must say the site did look a bit like the remains of a Roman villa – just the base and a few stubb walls peering above ground level, but at least it looked less like a disaster area hit by a tropical tsunami wave as it had when the pond and decapitated trees occupied the same spot. It really was quite encouraging.

A couple of evenings later we were enjoying a welcome glass of squash when a stranger walked onto the plot. It transpired that he was a site foreman for a local building company and apparently noticed our efforts right from the start; the pond being filled in – the tree felling, the trenches and now the oversite.

'See you're making good progress,' he smiled. 'It's good to see someone having a go at doing something for themselves. If you want any advice I would be delighted to help you, but don't ask me to lift a shovel or do any work.'

Malcolm and I exchanged glances. What an opportunity; someone experienced in the building trade and happy to give advice. We were more than happy to be doing the building work ourselves. A perfect arrangement. Over the next two years – the time it took to build our first house – this man's advice was very much appreciated.

It was Monday morning, the time 8.30 a.m. Malcolm had left for the factory in Aylesbury at 7.45, saying that he would arrange for a load of bricks to be delivered sometime during the day. No problem. I had plenty to keep me occupied for the rest of the day for sure and the bricks probably would not arrive until well after lunch. I had cleared the breakfast table, made the beds and put on the washing machine when there was a knock at the door. 'Ah, good morning, Mrs Baker?' the man in front of me asked.

'Um… yes,' I replied hesitantly.

'Oh good,' he said and gave me a lovely smile. 'I have your delivery of bricks.'

'But I wasn't really expecting any bricks until this afternoon,' I mumbled.

'Ah well, you see, your husband telephoned a brick order through at eight o'clock this morning and it just so happened a lorry had been loaded late yesterday afternoon for delivery today to another site, but they cancelled the order first thing this morning. So today is your lucky day.'

I was not so sure that it was my lucky day and the thought crossed my mind that it probably would not be the lorry driver's lucky day either.

'Where are you parked?' I asked.

'On the roadside at the end of your drive,' replied the red-haired lorry driver.

'Right. I'll just put on my Wellington boots and I'll show you where to unload them.'

Malcolm had decided that the bricks should be stacked against a large shed which backed onto the road. They would not look unsightly or take up precious space at the entry to the actual building site. Plus the fact that it would not be too much trouble to put the bricks into a wheelbarrow as and when we needed them and push the barrow across to the building plot, some fifty metres away.

I pulled on my boots and walked down to the parked lorry and showed the driver the shed and indicated that the bricks could be easily stacked against the base of the shed.

'That's fine,' he grunted, 'but where are the men?'

'What men?' I asked.

'The men from the site who are going to help me unload this lot,' said the lorry driver, pointing to the lorry-load of bricks. The smile had completely disappeared and it did not take many seconds for me to realise that I had been promoted (or was it demoted?) to the position of a lorry driver's 'brick unloader' assistant.

Back in the early sixties, pallets, portable hoists, mechanised unloaders or whatever you would care to call machinery that could shift a number of bricks with one lift, was just not readily available. So every brick had to be manhandled (or in this case, woman-handled) off the lorry and stacked neatly and carefully so that they did not take up too much space or become too damaged.

'No men here today – so I'll give a hand,' I replied with my biggest smile. The driver gave me a funny look and was obviously not very pleased with what he saw. One skinny housewife (I have always been a bit on the lean side) plus two and a half thousand bricks to be unloaded with care and no real help.

I would show the miserable blighter that I could unload just as quickly as he could, if not quicker. So I gave him another smile and walked towards the lorry.

'Come on then. We'd better get started, we can't hang around all day just looking at that load of bricks waiting to be unloaded, can we?'

A grunt was the only acknowledgment to the fact that he was prepared to help unload the bricks. He dropped the sides of the lorry and we were able to attack the bricks from all sides. It was only possible to carry six bricks at a time but we did not have to carry them any distance. It was surprising how quickly we moved them – stacking the majority of them in a tidy line against the full length of the shed about five feet high and ten feet deep; the remainder against the pine end of the shed. I started off working quite a lot faster then the driver, whose name was Jim.

'That's fine, my dear,' he said as I puffed past him with my tenth load to his eighth, 'but you won't keep that pace up.'

I just smiled. 'We'll see,' I said under my breath. My time spent mixing cement over the last few weeks had toughened me up quite a bit – but by the time we finished unloading, nearly two hours later, I was just about all in – not that I would admit that to anyone, especially a lorry driver.

The lorry stood empty and the shed now stood guard over a neat wall of building bricks. I was glad to see the back of the lorry as it was driven up the road but I was not going to sit down until it was completely out of sight. I did not want Jim the lorry driver to see me collapse in a heap on the lawn. His parting shot was 'Well, I've never had a woman to help me unload bricks before, but you did very well, considering'.

That was, I suppose, a sort of compliment.

By the time Malcolm returned from the factory that evening I had fully recovered and was eager to show him the rows of bricks. 'You'll be able to do some building with that little lot,' he smiled. 'Seriously, I think that you would enjoy the challenge. You could start on the pine end. It's a solid wall – no windows or doorways to cause you any problems. I can easily put up the insulation blocks for the internal wall any time. When the rest of the concrete blocks arrive, I can put up all the walls to divide the different rooms.' Malcolm made it all seem very simple.

'But how much cement between the bricks? How do I make sure all the levels are correct?'

'No problem. I'll show you. It's very easy really. We'll have a trial run tomorrow evening.'

I was very apprehensive. However, the following afternoon I threw the correct amounts of sand, cement and water into our newly-acquired cement mixer, which produced a good hefty barrow-load of perfect cement with which to make my first attempt at building a brick wall.

Malcolm arrived home promptly that evening. We had a quick bite, settled the children and were soon ready to start the evening's work. First Malcolm put wooden stakes into the ground at each end of the foundation slab. He then secured and stretched a piece of string between the stakes, which would be the guide to keep the bricks at the correct level as they were cemented into position. Cement was then placed near the edge of the foundation slab, in a neat, long, tidy pile; about a metre in length, two inches wide and one inch high (I still obviously had not come to grips with the metric system). A brick was then placed on top of the cement ridge, close to one of the wooden stakes, and a little pressure applied, which eased some cement out from under the brick. He then picked up another brick, applied cement to one end like a dollop of ice cream, and pushed it against the first brick; again a little cement peeped out. Malcolm very deftly removed the surplus and applied it to the end of another brick, which was placed in line with the others.

I was impressed.

'Right, now you have a go,' he said, handing me the trowel. So I did. A brick in my left hand, a dollop of ice cream cement smeared in a small pyramid on the end of the brick and placed against the brick that Malcolm had laid on the cement ridge; downward pressure until the cement oozed from under the brick; surplus cement removed; result – one brick laid on the wall.

'Fine' was the verdict. 'Lay one more,' came the instruction.

So I did.

'Right,' said Malcolm. 'You're well away. Just check your levels against the string, place the cement as evenly as possible and clear away any surplus before it sets too firmly.'

It was surprising how quickly the bricks covered the length of the wall. Malcolm then lifted the string level and checked it for the next course. To start with I would check the levels every third brick with a small spirit level, but it did not take long to learn the knack.

That evening I was quite pleased with my efforts; it was going to be quite a challenge but at least I was doing something constructive, and we could work together.

So a pattern was soon set in place. Most afternoons I would make sure that there were plenty of blocks, both insulation and concrete, for Malcolm to use, and plenty of bricks for me, with which to build up the one pine end, and of course a load of cement. It was a demanding project but we decided right at the beginning that we would not be slaves to this building lark. It was something that we could achieve and enjoy, but we also had three lively children to consider, now aged five years, eight years and nine years.

During the week the children were allowed to watch the children's programmes on television for one hour before our evening meal, which we would have as soon as Malcolm returned home from the factory. This was also a time when everyone could relate what they had been doing during the day. Always enlightening.

Then all three into the bath, followed by a story and into bed. Malcolm and I could then concentrate on the house building.

Most Friday evenings we would take the children swimming. At the weekend, depending on the weather, we would spend one day building and one day, or part of it, taking the children to a place of interest or on cycle rides. No prizes for guessing whose bicycle had the child seat for our five-year-old. It took us just over twelve months to complete the house and already we had someone knocking on the door to see when it would be put on the market.

After three years in Buckinghamshire we knew that it was pretty certain that Malcolm would be moved to another part of the country, possibly within the coming year. So we decided to sell the older, larger property that we had bought when we first moved into the village and move into the new smaller house. We told the lady who was interested in buying our project that she could have first refusal when it came on the market. She was delighted, especially as we thought that it would be within the next twelve months.

During the four years in the village we started a badminton club in the village hall and played tennis when we could. Bradley started school and by the age of seven had a great interest in chess and astronomy. There was no one, in his opinion, as good or as clever as Patrick Moore. I remember on the way to school one morning, Bradley asking me questions about Andromeda's spiral.

I could only just about spell the name of the famous constellation of stars, let alone know exactly where they were. They apparently spiral like the Milky Way and are the most remote objects easily visible to the naked eye. Strangely enough, we were on holiday in Gambia some thirty years later, having a meal in a hotel in Banjul, when we were asked if we would like to see the night sky through the new telescope that had been given to Gambia by the Royal Astronomical Society in England. The young man in charge of the telescope had met Patrick Moore in London whilst on a course on astronomy and was obviously a great fan. We joined a number of other folk to look at the stars and listen to the young man's commentary, which was fascinating and very informative. Then he said, 'As the sky is so clear tonight it will be very easy to pick out Andromeda's spiral.'

I could hardly believe my ears, but it was fascinating to see the format of the stars within the constellation some thirty years after first hearing the name of that spiral formation.

A very nice family bought the old hunting lodge and we moved into the smaller, newly-built house where we lived for one year before moving to Somerset where Malcolm took over a factory manufacturing baby foods and dairy products.

And so to Somerset. Another stepping-stone across the River of Life.